BACON
MOORE

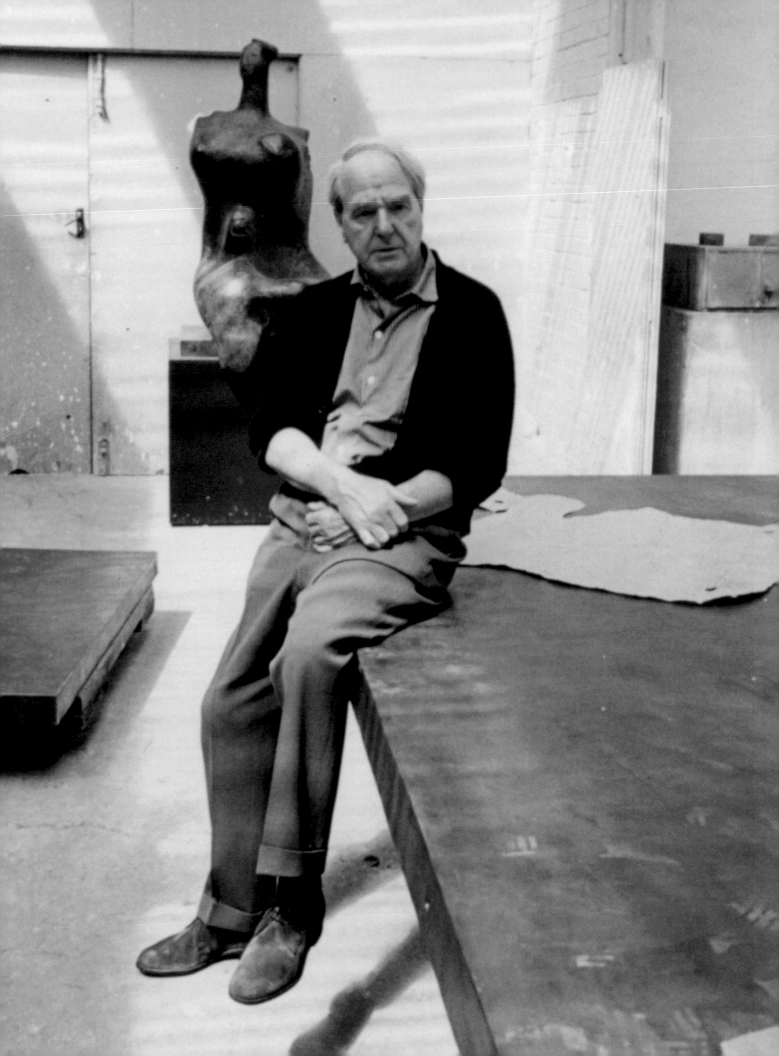

FRANCIS
BACON
HENRY
MOORE
FLESH
AND
BONE

ASHMOLEAN

LEAD SUPPORT OF THE EXHIBITION
HAS BEEN GENEROUSLY PROVIDED BY PICTET & CIE
WITH ADDITIONAL SUPPORT FROM
THE FRIENDS OF THE ASHMOLEAN
AND SOTHEBY'S

Bacon / Moore: Flesh and Bone
12 September 2013 to 5 January 2014
The Ashmolean Museum, Oxford

Richard Calvocoressi, Martin Harrison, and Francis Warner
have asserted their moral right to be identified as the authors of
this work.

British Library Cataloguing in Publications Data
A catalogue record for this book is available from the British Library

ISBN 978-1-85444-282-6 *paperback*
ISBN 978-1-85149-747-8 *hardback*

Catalogue designed and typeset in Brioni by Dalrymple
Printed and bound in Belgium by Deckers Snoeck

Front cover: *Portrait of Man with Glasses III* 1963,
by Francis Bacon (cat.57) Private Collection
Back cover: *Animal Head* 1951, by Henry Moore (cat.24)
The Henry Moore Foundation: gift of the artist, 1977
Frontispiece left: *Francis Bacon in his studio, London*, 1984,
photographed by Bruce Bernard
Frontispiece right: *Henry Moore in his studio, in front of* Woman
1957–8 (cat.35), *Perry Green*, 1967, photographed by Budd

For further details of Ashmolean titles please visit:
www.ashmolean.org/shop

Lenders to the Exhibition

The exhibition would not have been possible without
the generous support of the following:

The Estate of Francis Bacon

The Henry Moore Foundation

Charles Campbell

Christie's, London

Richard Clark Colton, Jr.

Hauser & Wirth

The Hepworth Wakefield

Leeds Art Gallery

New Walk Art Gallery and Museum, Leicester

Sainsbury Centre for Visual Arts, University of East Anglia

Tate

Mary Moore and the Henry Moore Family Collection

Museo de Bellas Artes de Bilbao

Pilar Ordovas

Pallant House, Chichester

Royal Pavilion and Museums, Brighton and Hove

Scottish National Gallery of Modern Art, Edinburgh

Ulster Museum, National Museums Northern Ireland

The Provost and Fellows of Worcester College, Oxford

And a number of private lenders who prefer
to remain anonymous

Director's Foreword

At first sight, the two greatest British artists of the twentieth century could not seem more different: Henry Moore, primarily a sculptor who also made superlative drawings; and Francis Bacon, a painter who rarely drew. Yet, unlike most of their contemporaries in this country, both artists concerned themselves with universal human truths, and, from their different perspectives, the ways in which the human figure can illustrate and exemplify those truths.

It is fifty years since the first joint exhibition of Henry Moore and Francis Bacon, at Marlborough Fine Art in London, which was followed by a second two years later. Since then, opportunities to compare their work have been limited to their inclusion in general surveys. The proposal by Richard Calvocoressi CBE, the Director of The Henry Moore Foundation, and Martin Harrison, editor of the Francis Bacon catalogue raisonné, to mount a carefully selected exhibition exploring the affinities between Bacon and Moore, was therefore most welcome. The two curators have worked tirelessly, not least in securing outstanding loans.

This is not the first time that the names of the two artists have been paired in Oxford: in 1970, Francis Warner, then a young English don at St Peter's College, gave a memorable lecture on 'Francis Bacon and Henry Moore' to the Oxford University Critical Society. We are delighted that Dr Warner, who was a friend of both artists, has contributed an essay to this catalogue, expanding on some of the themes of his original lecture.

Bacon Moore is one of the most ambitious exhibitions ever mounted in the Ashmolean. There is only a small handful of works by Moore in the collection, and none by Bacon, so we are especially indebted to the lenders, both public and private, who are listed opposite. The exhibition would not have been possible without substantial financial support. We are extremely pleased that Pictet & Cie, who sponsored our Westmorland exhibition in 2012, should once again be the lead sponsors for this exhibition, and very grateful to Stephen Barber and his colleagues for their continuing commitment to the Ashmolean. Additional support has been provided by the Friends of the Ashmolean and Sotheby's. Finally, we are very pleased that the exhibition will be seen in a modified form at the Art Gallery of Ontario in Toronto. Such a partnership furthers our commitment to bring the exhibitions and permanent collections in the Ashmolean to the widest possible audiences throughout the world.

PROFESSOR CHRISTOPHER BROWN CBE

Richard Calvocoressi

PROLOGUE

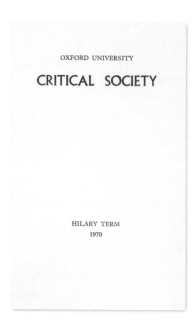

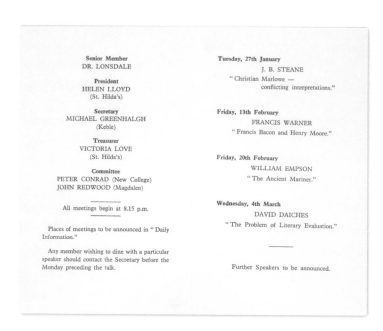

OXFORD UNIVERSITY

CRITICAL SOCIETY

HILARY TERM
1970

Senior Member
DR. LONSDALE

President
HELEN LLOYD
(St. Hilda's)

Secretary
MICHAEL GREENHALGH
(Keble)

Treasurer
VICTORIA LOVE
(St. Hilda's)

Committee
PETER CONRAD (New College)
JOHN REDWOOD (Magdalen)

All meetings begin at 8.15 p.m.

Places of meetings to be announced in " Daily Information."

Any member wishing to dine with a particular speaker should contact the Secretary before the Monday preceding the talk.

Tuesday, 27th January
J. B. STEANE
" Christian Marlowe —
conflicting interpretations."

Friday, 13th February
FRANCIS WARNER
" Francis Bacon and Henry Moore."

Friday, 20th February
WILLIAM EMPSON
" The Ancient Mariner."

Wednesday, 4th March
DAVID DAICHES
" The Problem of Literary Evaluation."

Further Speakers to be announced.

Fig.1 | Oxford University Critical Society, calendar, Hilary Term 1970 Private Collection

Since *Matisse Picasso* at Tate Modern in 2002, exhibitions bringing together giants of late-nine-teenth or twentieth century Western art have become relatively common. To cite just a few recent examples, in 2006 we had *Rodin and Picasso* at the Fondation Beyeler in Basel; in 2009, *Matisse and Rodin* at the Musée Rodin in Paris; while this year, 2013, has already seen *Bacon and Rodin* (Ordovas, London) and *Moore Rodin* (The Henry Moore Foundation, Perry Green).

The origins of this exhibition – in which Rodin, again, is an inescapable presence, albeit in the back-ground – lie in the Oxford of the early 1970s. When I went up to Oxford in the autumn of 1969 to read English, I joined the Museum of Modern Art (as it was then called), which offered a lively programme of talks and avant-garde films in addition to its exhibitions; and signed on for life drawing classes (three guineas a term) at the Ruskin School of Art, which in those days was housed in a wing of the Ashmolean Museum.

I also became a member of the Critical Society. The lecture which made the deepest impression on me was given to members of the society on 13 February 1970 by Francis Warner. A fellow and tutor in English literature at St. Peter's College, Francis was energetic and inspiring. He probably did more for the arts, especially the performing arts, in Oxford at that period than any other individual or organisation. His dream was to build an experimental theatre in the grounds of St. Peter's, named after Samuel Beckett and designed by Buckminster Fuller. He knew both playwright and architect well. I kept a copy of the appeal brochure, with its portraits of Beckett by his friend Avigdor Arikha, its goodwill message from Jennie Lee, Minister for the Arts, and a stellar list of supporters, including Benjamin Britten, Richard Burton, Maurice Bowra, Graham Greene, Peter Hall, Robert Lowell, Henry Moore, John Osborne, Harold Pinter, and John Piper, as well as Beckett's French, American and English publishers.

Francis's idea was to create 'a workshop for one

of the really great dramatists of our time' as well as 'a place where new playwrights from both sides of the Atlantic will be encouraged to experiment and perfect their craft'. The theatre would open with a complete cycle of Beckett's plays, one of which Beckett would himself produce, followed by new and experimental work by known and unknown dramatists. Francis was determined to provide a platform and financial support for the struggling avant-garde.

Sadly, the theatre was never built, but the money raised was invested, and now the Samuel Beckett Trust awards over £30,000 a year for experimental theatre productions. During the fundraising, Francis brought to Oxford some stars of stage and screen to give it their backing, among them Richard Burton and Elizabeth Taylor,[1] Laurence Harvey, and Helen Mirren, then a young actress with the Royal Shakespeare Company. For me, the most moving fundraising event was a performance at the Playhouse, for one night only, of Beckett's *Oh! Les Beaux Jours*, with Madeleine Renaud as Winnie and her husband Jean-Louis Barrault as Willie. Francis 're-directed' them in Roger Blin's original 1961 production. In the 1950s, Blin had also directed the first performances of *Waiting for Godot* and *Endgame*.

The subject of Francis's slide talk that evening was 'Francis Bacon and Henry Moore'. What I recall most clearly about it was Francis's conviction that both artists, having lived through two World Wars (in Moore's case, seeing active service in the first) and having experienced the Blitz (during which Bacon served in Air Raid Precautions), were engaged in a similar enterprise: restoring the human body, not to a state of perfection or even wholeness, but to a kind of dignified, animal resignation in the face of isolation and suffering. Conscious of mortality, each manages to convey an irrepressible sense of life. Their perspectives, of course, were different: Moore clung to a belief in humanism, while Bacon

espoused a post-humanist, nihilistic world view. And in expressing their visions of humanity, the two artists had very different approaches: Bacon working from the outside in, disintegrating and dissolving form; Moore from the inside out, pushing anatomical structure to the surface. Flesh and bone.

Francis knew both artists and was thus in an ideal position to compare their endeavours. In the summer of 1969 he and Harold Pinter invited Bacon to see a performance by the RSC in London of Pinter's new plays *Landscape* and *Silence*, followed by a quiet dinner for the three of them at a restaurant.

I know Mr Pinter would be as honoured as I would to see any pictures you had to show us. He works with nothing but reproductions of your work pinned up around his desk. I gave him the Marlborough-New York catalogue, but there is no substitute for the actual paintings.

Mr Samuel Beckett joins me in sending what really amounts to homage.[2]

On 8 March the following year, just three weeks after his lecture on Bacon and Moore, Francis staged the first performance in England of Beckett's *Breath* at the Playhouse, in aid of his planned theatre. At about thirty-five seconds in length, *Breath* is Beckett's shortest play –'the briefest play ever written', in Francis's words.

Breath is the ultimate distillation of the Noh. There is faint light on a stage littered with miscellaneous rubbish...Five second pause. Then a faint brief cry, a recorded instance of vagitus, the first cry of a new-born baby entering this world; and immediately an intake of breath (amplified), and slow increase of light and inspiration together reaching maximum together in about ten seconds. Then a five second silence. Then expiration and slow decrease of light together reaching minimum together in about ten

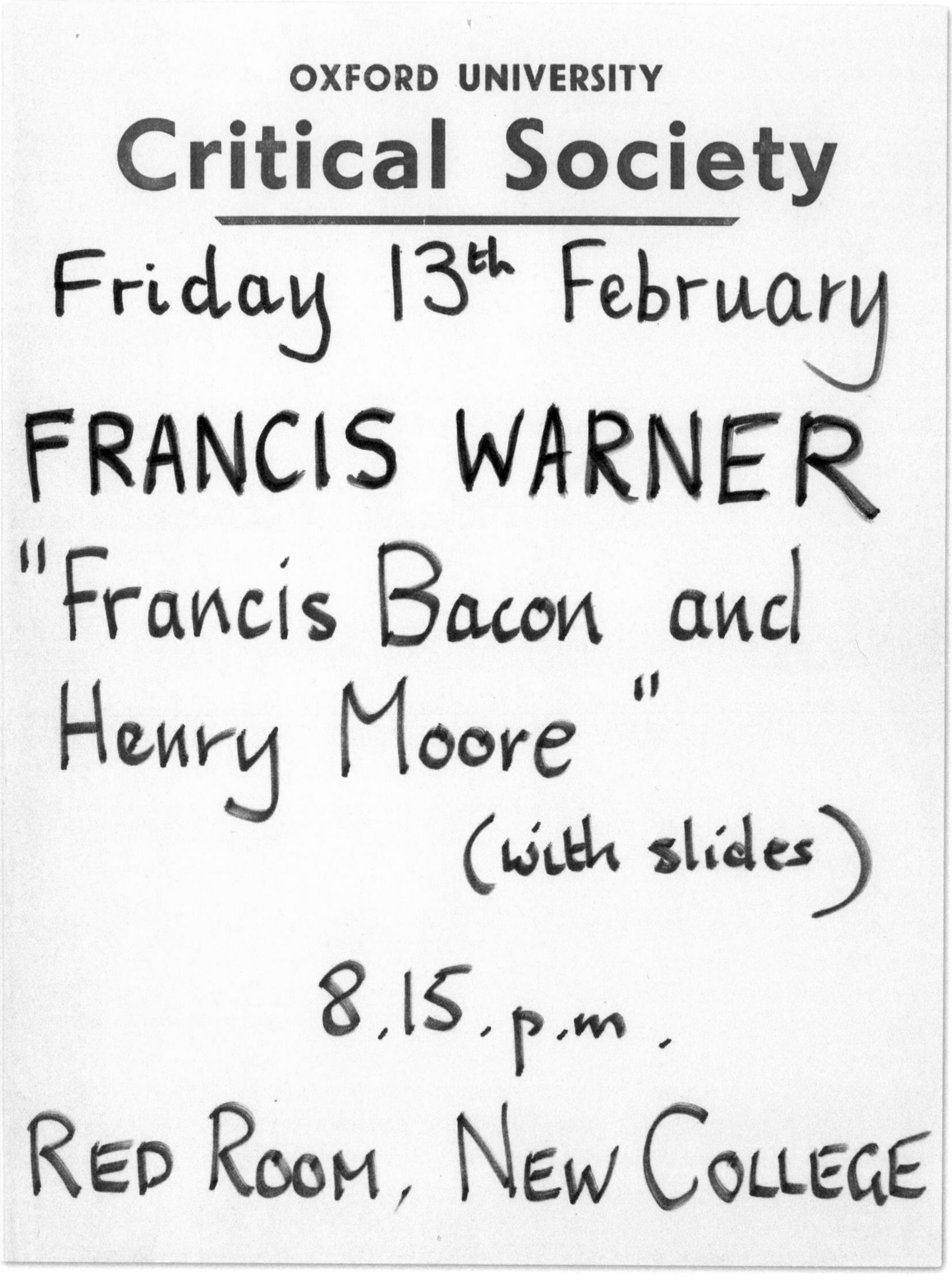

OXFORD UNIVERSITY
Critical Society

Friday 13th February
FRANCIS WARNER
"Francis Bacon and
Henry Moore"
(with slides)

8.15. p.m.
RED ROOM, NEW COLLEGE

Fig.2 | Oxford University Critical Society, poster for Francis Warner's talk, Hilary Term 1970, Private Collection

seconds and immediately the identical vagitus cry as before. Silence and hold for five seconds.

That is it.[3]

If *Breath* recalls the lines from T. S. Eliot's *Sweeney Agonistes* beloved of Bacon – 'Birth, and copulation, and death./That's all the facts when you come to brass tacks:/Birth, and copulation, and death.'[4] – it was Moore, not Bacon, who was in the audience, having dined with his party at the Elizabeth and met up with Warner at St Peter's before the performance.[5]

Since Francis Warner's lecture, it has always seemed to me perfectly natural that anyone would choose to think and talk about the work of Bacon and Moore together – a view enthusiastically shared by my collaborator, Martin Harrison. After all, Bacon and Moore had joint exhibitions in London in the 1960s, and the leading art critics of the day, including Andrew Forge, Bryan Robertson, John Russell, and Robert Melville, saw nothing unusual in this. But later generations of critics, art historians and museum curators have tended not to view their achievements as complementary. After their deaths – Moore in 1986, Bacon six years later – Moore's reputation suffered a decline, which has been reversed only in the last few years; while Bacon's, after a brief dip, gained continually in strength. Typical of the more sceptical attitude to Moore was the following reaction by Michael Peppiatt, who visited the sculptor a few years before his death.

For me as for many young people of my generation, Henry Moore lay like a monolith, both metaphorically and literally, across the landscape we grew up in. A backlash against such wholesale public recognition was inevitable. In becoming so dominantly Britain's Official Artist, Moore was now bound to stir up controversy of a very different kind. As an art critic who had been exposed to countless works by Moore,

I experienced not only a numbed response to roomfuls of unwieldy, gaping organic forms – often patently derivative of Picasso's bone sculpture – but a resentment at the implicit expectation that I would join unthinkingly in the widespread chorus of praise.[6]

Of course, reservations about Moore's status as one of the great and the good were nothing new. In 1967 forty-one British artists, including some of Moore's former assistants, had signed a letter to *The Times* objecting to the suggestion that the Tate Gallery was contemplating dedicating a large, permanent space to a proposed gift of his sculpture that Moore was discussing with the director and trustees.[7]

Not everyone, however, shared the 'numbed response' felt by Peppiatt. One notable critic who didn't was John Berger. Having regularly attacked Moore in the 1950s in his column in the *New Statesman*, Berger (who was no fan of Bacon either, although again he later recanted) published a sensitive, though not wholly uncritical, re-evaluation of Moore's work in 1989, three years after the artist's death. Berger praised Moore above all for introducing tactile experience into sculpture: a kind of pre-verbal, infantile sense – the child's experience of the mother's body – 'through an evocation of a special way of touching forms and being touched by them'. He concluded: '... the last period of Moore's working life – and notably the years when he was in his late 70s or over 80 – was of an incomparable richness. Here he joins the company of Titian or Matisse in the sense that his life's work becomes cumulative: his last works an apogee.'[8]

For those who thought they knew Henry Moore, the present exhibition may encourage them to look again (like Berger); and to discover, in the encounter with Francis Bacon, a powerful new dimension to the work of these two great artists.

Fig. 3 | *Auerbach – Bacon – Moore*, Marlborough Fine Art,
London, September 1979: installation view with (left)
Moore's *Large Four-Piece Reclining Figure* 1972–3 and (right)
Bacon's *Seated Figure* 1978

Richard Calvocoressi

MOORE AND BACON: AFFINITIES

A great deal can still be done with three-dimensional form as a means of expressing what people feel about themselves, and about nature, and about the world around them. But I don't think that we shall, or should, ever get far away from the thing that all sculpture is based on, in the end: the human body. HENRY MOORE, 1961[1]

In his journal entry for 23 May 1962, the poet and critic Stephen Spender recorded his reaction to the Francis Bacon retrospective at the Tate Gallery, which he had visited that day:

The paintings make horrifying statements with very great force. They are by an observer so profoundly affected by the kind of life he observes that, although protesting, they seem corrupted by the corruption. After Bacon most other contemporary painting seems decoration, doodling, aestheticism or stupidity. His work [is] extremely devoid of pleasure, perhaps this is partly due to the life of disillusionment he leads, which he faces in its implications; perhaps it is the old English puritanism and dislike of pleasure cropping up again.[2]

Over dinner a fortnight later, while talking about Raphael and Michelangelo, Bacon – still mourning the loss of his lover Peter Lacy who had died three weeks earlier – confided to Spender: 'My ambition would be to do something really beautiful and not ugly as all my paintings are, before I die.'[3]

Spender was also close friends with Henry Moore (fig.4). On 1 November 1979 he made notes for a talk on Moore's work:

He strikes me so much as being normal as a man that you might expect him to produce works of art which reflected one's conception of genial, sensible, brave, manly 'normality'. In fact he produces 'modern art'. But this is precisely because in our time the normal

is really the exceptional. Within the dehumanizing circumstances of modern life, a completely human art must do far more than create figures which are traditional or anatomically correct. The artist who is himself an intensely vital, energetic and energizing man has to establish and realize and uphold his individuality against the environment. In order to do this he has to absorb into himself some of the machine-like, beyond-the-human-scale characteristics of the age. A mother and child, or a reclining figure, or the most primitive of figures, have to absorb into themselves the strength of machines, whereby they can fortify their own humanity. This is what Moore does in his sculpture ...[4]

As these passages attest, Spender wrote thoughtfully about Moore and Bacon, whom he clearly judged to be in a class of their own.

In twentieth-century British art, as Spender intimated, Henry Moore and Francis Bacon had no equals. In their own different mediums, they created unforgettable images of the human figure, isolated in his or her environment, at once poignant and monumental. The distinctive visual languages which each developed over more than half a century were marked by a growing simplicity and grandeur of form. No other artists achieved such international reputations, and no other artists – with the exception of Richard Hamilton – were accorded two retrospectives at the Tate Gallery in their lifetime. Works by both are to be found in nearly all the important public collections in Europe, North America, Australia and Japan. In addition, as a sculptor working in the public domain, Moore's work remains familiar to millions through its permanent siting in cities and parks around the world.

Given that Moore and Bacon were both figurative artists with no religious faith, who nevertheless reimagined Christian themes – the Crucifixion

(Bacon and Moore), the Holy Family (Moore), the Madonna and Child (Moore) – for an increasingly secular, atrocity-conscious age, it is surprising that this is the first museum exhibition to compare their achievements. At a certain level, pairing these two giants of modern art may seem an unusual choice: the one a painter whose subject was flux, chance, the arbitrariness of existence; the other a sculptor who created universal symbols of strength and endurance. That, until recently, was the standard view of Moore, which the Moore exhibition at Tate Britain in 2010 set out to challenge by exposing a morbid and erotic side.[5] It should be noted, however, that in the Moore retrospective which he curated at the Tate in 1968, David Sylvester had earlier drawn attention to the underlying sexual imagery in much of Moore's work: oral and genital references, uterine associations, phallic shapes, and so on.[6]

The two artists were not close, had little in common in their personal lives, and took a very different view of honours, awards and official appointments.[7] Moore, the articulate and persuasive spokesman for sculpture as a public art, believed the artist had a responsibility to society; Bacon did not. Bacon was never very complimentary about Moore's work, dismissing his shelter drawings and making other pointed remarks in private.[8] In spite of this gulf between them, Maurice Ash, a friend of Moore's, recounted to the artist's biographer an incident in the 1950s when dinner at the Moores in Hertfordshire was delayed by over an hour while Moore spoke in private to 'a very agitated Bacon' who had turned up unexpectedly.[9] Francis Warner, who knew both artists, recalls Bacon asking him in the early 1970s if he could take sculpture lessons from Moore. Assuming it was serious – and this was certainly a time when Bacon was thinking deeply about making sculpture – nothing came of the proposal.[10]

The deeper we look into it, the more connections there are. Moore and Bacon were both born before the First World War, in which Moore was just old enough to serve in the trenches – an experience that was to have a profound, if delayed, effect on his work. Similarly, Bacon's consciousness of civil unrest in Ireland, where he spent part of his childhood and youth, introduced him, if not to the threat, then at least to the presence of violence at an early age. In the 1930s both artists were taken up by Douglas Cooper, the secretary of Unit One, a grouping of avant-garde artists and architects which included Moore. It was Cooper who persuaded Herbert Read to illustrate a recent painting by Bacon, *Crucifixion*, 1933, in his book *Art Now*, published a year before Read's 1934 monograph on Moore.[11] Both artists were influenced by surrealism at this date, but more especially by Picasso's biomorphic forms of the late 1920s, as the exhibition *Picasso and Modern British Art* at Tate Britain in 2012 demonstrated.[12]

Fig.5 | Moore sketching the coalminer Jack Hancock, Wheldale Colliery, Castleford, for the War Artists Advisory Committee, 1942

Fig.6 | Moore in Holborn Underground station, London, during the filming of *Out of Chaos*, about war artists, directed by Jill Craigie, September 1943

Fig.7 | Catalogue for group exhibition including Bacon and Moore, Lefevre Gallery, London, April 1945

During the Second World War, both men lived through the Blitz, Bacon as an ARP Warden, Moore as an official war artist (figs 5, 6). As war ended, a group exhibition opened at the Lefevre Gallery in London in which Bacon showed his *Three Studies for Figures at the Base of a Crucifixion,* 1944, propelling him into the limelight for the first time (fig.7). It is often overlooked that in the same exhibition Moore showed two sculptures from the 1930s and fourteen wartime drawings, some of which anticipate the theme – though not the savage imagery – of Bacon's triptych.

The practice of exhibiting together in a commercial gallery was repeated in the 1960s and 1970s when Moore and Bacon were both represented by Marlborough Fine Art. In the summers of 1963 and 1965, for example, the Marlborough New London Gallery held joint exhibitions of their work (Figs 8, 13). These shows, extensively reviewed in the press, gave critics the perfect chance to compare the artists'

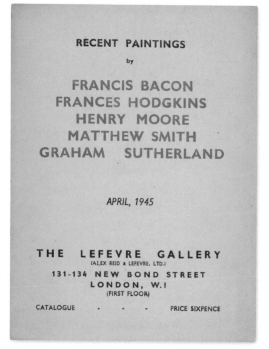

RECENT PAINTINGS

by

FRANCIS BACON
FRANCES HODGKINS
HENRY MOORE
MATTHEW SMITH
GRAHAM SUTHERLAND

APRIL, 1945

THE LEFEVRE GALLERY
(ALEX REID & LEFEVRE, LTD.)
131-134 NEW BOND STREET
LONDON, W.1
(FIRST FLOOR)

CATALOGUE · · · PRICE SIXPENCE

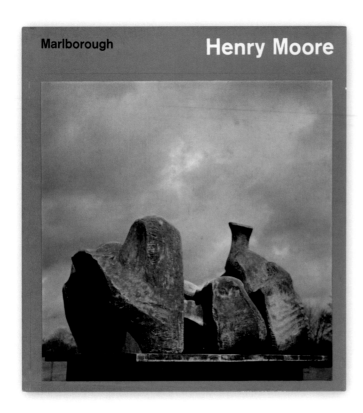

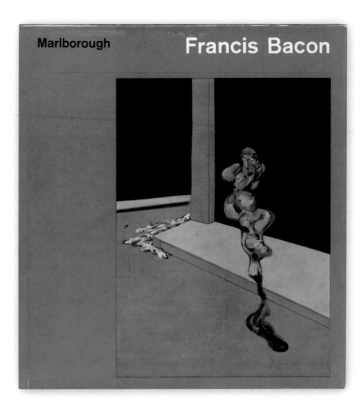

radical approaches to the human form, which were by and large seen as complementary rather than conflicting. Reviewing the 1963 exhibition (nineteen sculptures by Moore, thirteen paintings by Bacon, all from the previous three years), Myfanwy Piper wrote that Moore 'never forgets the solidity of flesh upon the bone, the strength of the bone beneath the flesh', while Bacon 'never forgets that flesh is meat'.

Whatever Moore does to the human body ... he never seriously questions its dignity. The end is resolved in peace, a calm sensual resignation to life and to death, at once committed and detached from the implications of both, like the smiling figures of Etruscan funeral caskets. He has found a way of honouring our liking (and his own) for a classical voluptuousness of form without cloying by imitation or denying the accidents and pressures of the twentieth century ...

What saves [Bacon's] paintings from being a series of gimmicks ... is that he is really no more of a literary artist than Henry Moore is. What he wants to do can only be done in paint ... They are visual comments on states of being, moments of desperation, changes of physical appearance caught at the moment of dissolving, a confusion of flesh and soul ... the antithesis of classical art, it is still pure in its loyalty to paint.[13]

The *Times* art critic described the experience of moving 'from the boniness of Moore's sculpture ... to the bonelessness of Bacon's figures' (fig.9):

Their convulsive deformations may still at times seem horrifying, the models occasionally the victims of dire catastrophe. But Bacon paints them now in a tempestuously virtuoso style, fragmenting them and reassembling the fragments in a more involved organic whole, like some sort of cubism which instead of angles and planes uses scooped, circling, spiralling brushstrokes loaded with fleshy pigment.[14]

Nevile Wallis in the *Spectator* felt that Bacon's figures were 'as fully plastic as Daumier's' and that 'most significant now is the full sinuous amplitude of the forms which makes Bacon's next step to sculpture seem inevitable'.[15] In the *Listener*, Bryan Robertson also made the connection with sculpture – 'many of these bunched up, convulsive figures might also stem from the early sculptures of Matisse' – but found Bacon's vision, as distinct from Moore's, restricted (fig.10): 'He [Bacon] is not making a tragic image. Instead, he is playing out a morbid – not tragic – obsession which has meaning within the terms of psychopathology, but can never attain the universality of genuine tragedy ...'.[16]

Writing in the *New Statesman*, Andrew Forge had no such reservations:

"Three Piece Reclining Figure", 1961-62, by Henry Moore.

New Work by Henry Moore and Francis Bacon

From Our Art Critic

The concurrence of recent work by Mr. Henry Moore and Mr. Francis Bacon in one and the same gallery promised to be quite a formidable occasion, and so it proves. The entrance alone to the exhibition at the *New London Gallery*, 17-18, *Old Bond Street*, which takes one past two giant Moore bronzes, one an arch shaped like a pelvic bone, the other resembling the sort of towering rock-face in which prehistoric cliff-dwellings are found, supplies as unnerving a demonstration of sculptural power as one wants to experience in any confined space.

Moore has never looked grander, more inventive, more the absolute master of his means of expression. Bone-shapes are now almost the whole source of his formal vocabulary, but they are no

Study for a head, 1962, by Francis Bacon.

longer as literally transcribed (they are, that is to say, no longer as baldly bony) as when he started on them a couple of years ago, but serve whatever mood or characteristic weight of allusion he wants them to carry. As a more than worthy successor to his famous "two-piece" reclining figures, he now shows one in three sections based on the shapes of vertebrae. Whereas the two-piece figures suggested sea-caves and marine headlands, the pieces wrested apart as by a convulsion of the elements, the new figure is more like the tumbled, wind-eroded boulders of some desert range of hills, brooded over by a head like a watching vulture's.

This majestic, superbly articulated invention contrasts with two others which are purely abstract and in which Moore, smoothing and polishing the surface of his bronze as he has not done for a long time, seems to recall something of his finest carvings in polished stone of the 1930s. One, "Locking piece", does what it says, turning on itself in a marvellous sequence of entwined planes. The other, "Knife-edge two-piece", is remarkable not only in its flow of surface and contour but in the exceptional beauty of its patina. Anyone, incidentally, interested in the workings of the creative mind will be enthralled by a little collection of pebbles, bones, shells, and clay models from the sculptor's workshop which is also on view.

From the boniness of Moore's sculpture, one moves through to the bonelessness of Bacon's figures. Their convulsive deformations may still at times seem horrifying, the models occasionally victims of dire catastrophe. But Bacon paints them now in a tempestuously virtuoso style, fragmenting them and reassembling the fragments in a more involved organic whole, like some sort of cubism which instead of angles and planes uses scooped, circling, spiralling brushstrokes loaded with fleshy pigment. The rolling curves both in the figures and even more in the distorted perspective of their settings produce a curious sensation of instability and *mal-de-mer*, but it is an effect induced less by the imagery itself than by a new assertion of style in the compositions.

In these paintings Bacon isolates and encloses his standing, turning, or seated figures as much as he ever did in glass cages, but he tends to put them now in an area like that of a completely circular room. There are some new colours—shrill, violet, strong blues, and white—but in the way they create a more specific kind of picture-space, however ambiguous, a disturbing jump in style between setting and figure is sometimes involved. Even if the intention is to contrast something static with something that moves, the effect is of an uneasy transition between slightly exploratory and wholly confident styles of performance. But if some paintings in this exhibition seem not wholly resolved, there are several—notably the "Turning Figure No. 3", "Study for portrait of P.L.", the extraordinary "Landscape near Malabata, Tangier", and some small portrait heads that once or twice have the look of a Daumier—in which Bacon's uncanny power and skill manifest themselves to the full.

Moore and Bacon

By BRYAN ROBERTSON

BACON'S recent paintings at the New London Gallery show as clearly as ever that he is projecting an image of death from which all positive life or hope is rigorously excluded. That is the point of his work and its fatal restriction. He is not making a tragic image. Instead, he is playing out a morbid—not tragic—obsession which has meaning within the terms of psychopathology, but can never attain the universality of genuine tragedy, for this needs an alternative ingredient to offset its negation and provide the real catharsis that we find in Mantegna, Rembrandt, and Goya. The horror of absolute corruption, brought almost to the edge of death, is hermetically sealed in Bacon's work and clings on, sick and fearful, in a self-absorbed trance. The painting itself is bold and energetic, but undermined by the weaknesses of expressionist rapportage intent upon registering *feeling* in terms of paint without any constructive *thought* to push the paint further. And so the formal qualities of his figures and backgrounds are rarely successful, and even then only at an elementary level. The compression chamber, the intangible prison cell, so familiar from literature, has lost its meaning and turns into a sentimental device.

There is still much to admire. The drips of paint, used as a perspective device to pinpoint space, which still carry an emotional weight. The tightrope tension between specific, readable reality, and camouflaged, out of focus areas of activity—objects on the edge of the arena, or the visceral black splayed across parts of the figures. The insistence on *vertical* figures—consistent for many years—even when foreshortened and recumbent, to produce an active, bristling immediacy of contact with the spectator, who is almost trapped as a protagonist. (The standing figure in the street was originally a reclining figure.) The equally consistent alienation effect achieved by the scale of figure to space or furniture; the cut-out figure from one canvas superimposed on another; or the two figures in 'Man and Child' in which the child's legs are separated from her body by placing the figure against the diagonal, disrupting intersection of wall and floor while the man's head and shoulders are isolated from his body by being set against a window frame. The familiar preoccupation with furniture as an active participant, changing according to the formal tensions of the figures. The obvious approach to sculpture, for many of these bunched up, convulsive figures might almost stem from the early sculptures of Matisse when he was trying to bring a baroque amplitude into the severities of cubism, or the sculpture

of Duchamp-Villon. And the sensuous resolution of individual passages in the painting—this can be beautiful, as in the drifting debris in the street scene. There is much else to be absorbed by and to admire, but the severe limitations rob these works of complete authority. Disparities in scale between figure and

'Turning Figure' by Francis Bacon and (*right*) 'Seated Woman' by Henry Moore: from the exhibition of their work at Marlborough New London Gallery, 17-18 Old Bond Street, London, W.1

context may occasionally have a point as psychological impact, but too often are clearly the result of weak design, as in the feeble 'Figure with Hypodermic Syringe'. There is also the disagreeable feeling that something repellent is being gilded, prettified, in a *chic* sense—a hunk of raw, putrefying meat in a smart, bright décor. The colour itself remains arbitrary, and the lighter tones lack an earlier resonance. Design has expanded slightly and comments on certain aspects of abstract art, but they are only used, coldly, they are not explored. In this sense, and in others, Bacon's work belongs to the academy, and relies more and more on sentimental sensationalism.

We are left with the personal myth and the *performance* as an artist. Both are fascinating and in different ways command respect. The myth has absolute validity, based as it is on courage, independence, and a high degree of professional energy shot through by ambiguities of technique and formal irresolutions. Bacon's shortcomings are those of any artist crippled by an excessively self-indulgent obsessive vision. Outside that, out in the world, only a handful of people can truthfully respond, though they can stare through lurid shock. For his work has not made a world with real meaning for any possible society, but only a morbid aspect of what is anti-life, a painful travesty ritual on the razor's edge of death. Trapped there, it is incapable of growth, only an occasional increase in confidence at a fixed level.

The new sculpture of Henry Moore confirms a feeling that after marking time for a while in the nineteen-fifties he has moved through to an intensity of feeling and constructive energy which

p.t.o.

Fig.8 | *Henry Moore* and *Francis Bacon* exhibition catalogues, Marlborough New London Gallery, summer 1963.
The catalogues were contained within a transparent plastic wallet, back to back

Fig.9 | Review of Moore and Bacon exhibition, *The Times*, 12 July 1963

Fig.10 | Bryan Robertson, review of Moore and Bacon exhibition, *The Listener*, 25 July 1963

2 Francis Bacon Three Studies for Portrait of Lucian Freud 1964

23 Henry Moore Reclining Figure 1931

Bacon represents by an extraordinary and baffling process and it is here that the strength and mystery of his art lies, and not in the dramas that are so easily improvised round his subjects. It reverses every familiar pictorial sequence: it is the opposite of traditional painting ... He doesn't offer an essence of an appearance but the opposite, whatever that might be: something like a pile of clinker from which the essence has long since been burned out.

Forge noticed a striking change in Moore's work:

The old pebbly consistency of form has given way to something far more strenuous. Sharpness is poised against fullness, round maternal shapes are twisted against bone, fine precise surfaces are juxtaposed to masses swelling up from the centre ...

As you move round the figures, the image reconstitutes itself continually, becomes alert where you had taken it to be blunt, massively strong where it had seemed most fined down.

But it was the juxtaposition of the two artists' recent work that Forge found so illuminating:

The exhibition at the New London Gallery is the most memorable showing by two English artists that I have ever seen. This is so not only because of the quality

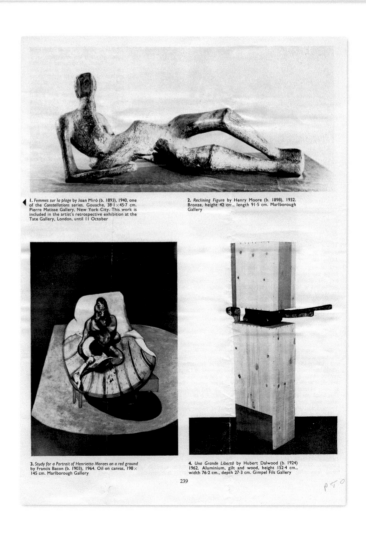

1. *Femmes sur la plage* by Joan Miró (b. 1893), 1940, one of the Constellations series. Gouache, 38·1×45·7 cm. Pierre Matisse Gallery, New York City. This work is included in the artist's retrospective exhibition at the Tate Gallery, London, until 11 October

2. *Reclining Figure* by Henry Moore (b. 1898), 1932. Bronze, height 42 cm., length 91·5 cm. Marlborough Gallery

3. *Study for a Portrait of Henrietta Moraes on a red ground* by Francis Bacon (b. 1903), 1964. Oil on canvas, 198 × 145 cm. Marlborough Gallery

4. *Una Grande Libertà* by Hubert Dalwood (b. 1924) 1962. Aluminium, gilt and wood, height 152·4 cm., width 76·2 cm., depth 27·3 cm. Gimpel Fils Gallery

239

Fig.11 | *Aspects of 20th Century Art*, Marlborough New London Gallery, summer 1964, catalogue spread illustrating works by Bacon and Moore

Fig.12 | *Apollo*, September 1964, with illustrations of works by Moore and Bacon

Fig.13 | *Francis Bacon* and *Henry Moore* exhibition catalogues, Marlborough New London Gallery, summer 1965. The catalogues were contained within a transparent plastic wallet, back to back

of the works but also because of the insight that it affords into Moore's and Bacon's development ...

It is a wonderful juxtaposition ... They are at extreme poles and there is grandeur in the contrast between them: Moore's timelessness, his authoritative, silent, female warmth, the acrid masculinity of Bacon's images, counting their minutes. It is like a vast résumé of what art can encompass. But the affinities between them are just as meaningful. What more precious lesson about the sources of art than in the example of their commitment to their subject-matter? Certain affections, obsessively held, regulate everything they do. They stalk their internal quarries implacably. They seem to be familiar with their own innermost recesses, to understand without anxiety the connection between their fantasies and the forms they can make with their hands.[17]

The following year Marlborough held a mixed exhibition, *Aspects of Twentieth-Century Art*, in which, as the art critic of *Apollo* noted, 'Moore and Bacon confront each other' (figs 11 and 12):

The intensity with which Bacon can express revulsion for flesh and the ignoble aspects of man is emphasised by Moore's monumentalizing of the human form so that it expresses the permanency of landscape shapes.

Henry Moore's "Three Way Piece: Archer 1964," from the exhibition of his work at the Marlborough New London Gallery. This bronze, which is 24in high, has not previously been exhibited.

MAGICIANS OF ART CAN STILL CAUSE SURPRISE

MOORE & BACON EXHIBITION

By TERENCE MULLALY

TWO of the magicians of contemporary British art, Henry Moore and Francis Bacon, prove in their latest exhibition that they can still surprise us. It continues at the Marlborough New London Gallery, 17, Old Bond Street, until the end of August.

Several of the Moores were recently seen at the Tate. Others are on view for the first time, and all the Bacons are new.

Moore, in a note prefixed to his part of the catalogue, says: "I don't think that we shall, or should, ever get far away from the thing that all sculpture is based on in the end: the human body."

Yet he has moved further from the human figure than ever before.

In his vast "Reclining Figure Three Piece: Bridge Prop 1963," which dominates the exhibition, the reference to the human body, although tenuous, is still unmistakable.

The same is not true of the latest works, "Three Way Piece: Archer 1964" and "Three Way Piece: Points 1964." Compared with the small bronzes of the past, included in the exhibition, they seem a retrogressive step.

Untouched by hope

Bacon is, if anything, moving in the opposite direction. His involvement with man's dilemmas is more brutal, more uncompromising, than ever before.

The force of his images is untouched by any redeeming humanity or hope. Even the two kneeling figures in his "Crucifixion" appear as a cruel commentary on the ordinary.

It is as though not content with flaying his own soul, Bacon is determined to leave the rest of us no refuge. His latest work wreaks of the corruption of the flesh.

Yet despite all the pictorial ingenuity, and force, we remain not deeply touched. Neither Bacon nor events can quite kill hope.

Tranquil, solid and confident of their supremacy over fleeting and destructive emotions, his figures embody the spirit of eternity, while Bacon's embody transitory states and mortality. Both sides of the coin need to be shown.[18]

In the summer of 1965 the renewed opportunity to see a substantial group of work by both artists in the same (albeit partitioned) space at Marlborough was singled out by the critics as being equally revealing: 'Bacon and Moore again in Powerful Relation' was the headline of the *Times* review of 14 July 1965. The exhibition contained nine new paintings by Bacon, including his *Crucifixion* triptych of 1965 (now in the Pinakothek der Moderne in Munich), as well as twenty-five sculptures and ten works on paper by Moore (fig.13). The sculptures covered the period between 1951 and 1964, and included two large bronzes, *Three Piece Reclining Figure No. 2: Bridge Prop*, 1963, and *Atom Piece (Working Model for Nuclear Energy)*, 1964–5. Writing this time in the *Spectator*, Bryan Robertson was kinder to Bacon, applying to his new pictures an insight by Moore (published in the catalogue) in which he praises the sculptures of Giovanni Pisano for being 'static and dynamic at the same time':

His [Bacon's] figures are static and dynamic in the way that movement, momentary distortion, the sensation of an after-image, or the vertiginous swirl of an elliptically curved room is accentuated by the flow of movement coursing through its three isolated occupants ...

This is arguably Bacon's most impressive exhibition ...

The atmosphere of objectified despair in his work, entranced and nihilistic, is trapped in those timeless pressure-chambers still more disquietingly. Moore's invincible sense of human resilience ... is sometimes frozen into hard, wary monumentality as in the recent *Bridge Prop* reclining figure, but his surrealist instinct makes it hard to tell hot from cold, flesh from bone, helmet or shell from leathery skin.[19]

In the *New Statesman*, Robert Melville remarked on Bacon's closeness to sculpture, 'as if he were modelling faces and bodies out of wet clay'.[20] Reviewing the show for *The Sunday Times*, John Russell (who wrote monographs on both artists) observed something similar:

Fig.15 | *Henry Moore Sculpture 1950 –1960*, Whitechapel Art Gallery, November – December 1960: Moore and Bryan Robertson (director) with *Warrior with Shield* 1953–4, *Two-Piece Reclining Figure No. 1* 1959, and (foreground) *Falling Warrior* 1956–7 (cat.32)

Fig.16 | Bryan Robertson and Moore admiring a phallic-looking *Two-Piece Reclining Figure No. 1*, Whitechapel Art Gallery, 1960

Both Moore and Bacon have always known to evoke, obliquely or directly, the blind and irrational forces which are at work in the world.[21]

Certainly the post-war work of both artists was affected by the revelations of Nazi atrocities – Bacon's perhaps more explicitly than Moore's. In the 1950s Moore became a close friend of Constantine FitzGibbon, his neighbour in Hertfordshire and an expert on the Third Reich. FitzGibbon accompanied him to Auschwitz in 1958 when Moore was invited to chair an international sculpture competition for a memorial to the camp's victims.[22] The FitzGibbons were also friendly with Bacon.

Not surprisingly, the term 'tragic' was used to describe the work of both artists. Robert Melville, for example, noticed

that whenever the tragic element appears in twentieth-century painting clear analogies with Christian iconography arise: Picasso's *Guernica* has an angel of pity, Francis Bacon's most painful images gyrate around the crucifixion ... and those works which constitute Moore's most magnificent pictorial achievement – *Four Grey Sleepers*, *Two Sleepers*, *Pink and Green Sleepers* [a reference to the shelter drawings] – explore once more the theme of the sleeping disciples in the Garden of Olives. Reality clarifies and simplifies the dream.[23]

In 1960 Bryan Robertson organized a large exhibition of Moore's sculpture of the previous ten years at the Whitechapel Art Gallery, of which he was director (figs 15, 16). Before Moore had agreed to the proposal, Robertson told him that his ambition was 'to make the installation of your exhibition the most perfect and thrilling thing of its kind ever tackled in London' and that he had 'many ideas for it – mostly of extreme simplicity'.[24] In his catalogue introduction, Robertson also linked the tragic dimension in Moore's work – a

A year ago ... Bacon was said to be turning to sculpture. Today, seeing his 'Three Figures in a Room' triptych, we realise that he doesn't need to: the sculpture is there already, in the paintings ...

The show reminds us ... that the dynamic behind Moore and the dynamic behind Bacon have this in common: that the re-invention of the human body is common to both ...

dimension in which he would later criticize Bacon for being deficient, as we have seen – to Christian imagery:

His [Moore's] work is grim, and on occasion tragic. There is no easy reassurance in it ... Look ... at the *Three Vertical Motives* of 1955–6 with the Glenkiln Cross as their centre piece [cat.31], and we find that architectural and organic, Christian and pagan elements are combined in a fierce image that does not attempt to resolve itself in synthesis. There are intimations of a figure that is a cross and a cross that is also a figure. The meaty, stump-like shapes and the vagaries of weathered incision and indentation do not comfort us. They are exceedingly disturbing. Here is a dramatic and tragic image and only ancient Celtic art can approach it in comparable mystery and grandeur ...

Moore has chosen to express his sense of the tragedy and essential nobility of life, as he feels it, in a long series of archetypal images which transcend life ... And yet his archetypal images, for all their passing references to art, are filled with life: everything that Moore touches has a living presence.[25]

It is no accident that the majority of Moore's sculptures in the present exhibition date from the 1950s, when the artist's output in bronze increased dramatically but before he started to enlarge his figures beyond normal human dimensions. As Alan Bowness has written, 'the extraordinary impact of the *Falling Warrior* of 1956–7 [cat.32] derives from the half-conscious connection we immediately make between his fall and the idea of being ourselves in the same situation'.[26] In the early part of his career Moore was primarily a carver. The doctrine of 'truth to material', of 'direct carving' in order to respect the character of stone or wood and reveal its particular qualities, was paramount. After World War Two, however, Moore turned increasingly to bronze casting. He found that he could model and carve plaster for a bronze in a

quarter of the time it took him to carve a sculpture in stone or wood. It also enabled him to work on a much bigger scale. He liked bronze as a material. 'The special quality of bronze is that you can reproduce with it almost any form and any surface texture through expert casting', he once said. 'Bronze can do anything'.[27] Moore was unusual in that he took a keen interest in the various stages of the casting process, often working on the sculpture's surface after patination so that the bronze would show through again.

Moore's first retrospective at the Tate, in 1951, consisted of seventy-two sculptures and ninety-seven drawings. Of the sculptures, only twenty-four, or exactly a third, were bronzes or their originals in terracotta or plaster. By 1968, the date of his second retrospective, the balance had swung in favour of bronze: two-thirds, or ninety sculptures out of a total of one hundred and forty-four, were in bronze, plaster or terracotta. Both exhibitions were selected, at Moore's request, by David Sylvester, arguably the leading art critic of his day by the late 1960s (fig.17). As a young man in his early twenties, Sylvester had worked briefly as Moore's part-time secretary at the end of the war, gaining his trust and respect. In addition to selecting the two Tate shows, he edited two volumes of the Moore catalogue raisonné and conducted a number of interviews with the sculptor: most notably for the BBC in 1963, a version of which was printed in the catalogue of the show which Moore shared with Bacon at Marlborough that year; and for *The Sunday Times Magazine* in 1964, when they discussed the work of Michelangelo.

In the context of the present exhibition, Sylvester's 1968 Tate catalogue is of cardinal significance. It was Sylvester who first commented that Moore's reclining women are 'more male than female'[28] – a sexual ambiguity which relates them to the series of Rodin-inspired reclining figures painted by Bacon between 1959 and 1961. In the catalogue

Fig.17 | David Sylvester and Moore standing in front of a cast of *Upright Motive No.7* 1955–6 (cat.31) during the installation of Moore's retrospective at the Tate Gallery, photographed by Martine Franck, 1968

Rodin's influence is evident in the fluid, melting parts of the *Upright Motives*. But the crucial influence has been Michelangelo ...

The development of these contrasts represents a radically new way of thinking for Moore – an emphasis on dynamic rather than static qualities, and on the uneasy rather than the harmonious.[30]

And he quotes Moore as saying:

'This is, perhaps, what makes me interested in bones as much as in flesh, because the bone is the inner structure of all living form. It's the bone that pushes out from inside ... And so the knee, the shoulder, the skull, the forehead, the part where from inside you get a sense of pressure of the bone outwards – these for me are the key points'.[31]

Sylvester's concluding analysis is especially perceptive:

Underlying this new concern is a new extreme concentration on tactile and motor rather than visual sensations – on what is experienced in running one's hands over a body, responding more sharply to its hardnesses and softnesses, its hollows and bumps, than when looking at them, and on what is experienced in using one's own body, feeling one's skin stretching tautly over one's knuckles as one clenches a fist, feeling the muscles tighten as one extends a limb. The hard-and-soft figures are haptic images: they make bodies look the way they feel, from outside, and, still more perhaps, from inside. To the eye they can seem dislocated, awkward, uncouth. They ask to be looked through, rather than at. In no other works has Moore taken such risks. And this reflects a further change of attitude – a growing acceptance, indeed, a positive courting, of imperfection, incompleteness.[32]

Moore's increasing preference for the unfinished and fragmentary in sculpture is directly related to his

section entitled 'Hard and Soft', Sylvester observed a fundamental change that had come over Moore's work in about 1955: 'Moore quite suddenly started to do sculptures in which there are violent contrasts of surface tension, with exceedingly taut, bone-hard, passages moving into soft, resilient, fleshy passages, often very abruptly.'[29]

As examples of the new hard/soft contrast, Sylvester cites the *Three Upright Motives* of 1955–6, *Falling Warrior*, 1956–7, and *Woman*, 1957–8 – all three sculptures in the current exhibition (cats 31, 32, 35). He goes on to attribute this shift in Moore's work to his 'having come to work mainly in plaster – modelling followed by the carving of a relatively soft material':

appreciation of Michelangelo, which he had articulated in 1957 in his seminal text 'The hidden struggle':

There is one quality I find in all the artists I admire most – men like Masaccio, Michelangelo, Rembrandt, Cézanne. I mean a disturbing element, a distortion, giving evidence of a struggle of some sort ...

Art and life are made up of conflicts.

I think really that in great art, i.e., in the art I find great, this conflict is hidden, it is unsolved. Great art is not *perfect*. Take the Rondanini Pietà, one of the greatest works of Michelangelo. It is not a perfect work of art. There is a huge arm remaining from the earlier statue which was later changed into the Pietà. It has nothing to do with the composition. Nevertheless, it was left there ...[33]

By the mid-1950s Moore's resistance to the classical and Renaissance tradition, in favour of revivifying the language of sculpture by reworking archaic, primitive and non-European styles, had been overcome. His growing fascination with the Parthenon (or Elgin) Marbles and other classical antiquities in the British Museum, and his revelatory visit to Greece in 1951 (fig.18) inspired a change in his sculptures, characterized by the introduction of figures clothed in rippling drapery, a preoccupation with asymmetry, and an increasing need for the sculpture to be seen in the round – something he would also take from Rodin.[34]

The 1950s saw the publication of several books on Michelangelo, such as Ludwig Goldscheider's *Michelangelo Drawings* (1951), Johannes Wilde's *Italian Drawings in the Department of Prints and Drawings in the British Museum: Michelangelo and his Studio* (1953), and Adrian Stokes's *Michelangelo: A Study in the Nature of Art* (1956). Moore acquired all three soon after they appeared. In his copy of Goldscheider he flagged the following images: studies of arms, hands and twisting bodies for the Sistine ceiling frescoes; sketches for the Raising of Lazarus;

studies for a Thief on the Cross; studies of torsos and legs for the Medici Chapel sculptures *Night* and *Day*; sketches of a male torso, a Christ on the Cross and a Holy Family; and two mother and child drawings.

Moore may also have been influenced by his friend and patron Kenneth Clark, whose book *The Nude*, published in 1956, concludes with a couple of pages on Moore's reclining figures. In Clark's chapter on 'Pathos', we read the following: 'Antique art has come down to us in a fragmentary condition, and we have virtuously adapted our taste to this necessity ... We have come to think of the fragment as more vivid, more concentrated and more authentic.'[35]

As examples of pathos in Michelangelo's work, Clark cites his last three *Pietàs*, including the Rondanini *Pietà*, and his late Crucifixion drawings.

Much of the 1964 *Sunday Times Magazine*

Fig.19 | Double-page spreads from Moore's interview with David Sylvester about Michelangelo, *Sunday Times Magazine*, 16 February 1964

The *Crucifixion* drawings are very simplified, without the twisting and turning of the earlier Michelangelo, yet they have a slight movement, a slight hang and turn that gives a sense of agonised weight. All his past experience is in them.[36]

A few years before his death Moore made three Crucifixion drawings, all inspired by Michelangelo and one of them clearly based on his *Christ on the Cross between the Virgin and St John*, c.1555–64, in the British Museum. It was a moving homage from one who had all but stopped making sculpture (cat.43). Moore would have known the reproductions of Michelangelo's late Crucifixion drawings in his copies of Goldscheider and Wilde. However, he was evidently familiar with two of them, including the Ashmolean sheet, long before the 1950s, having owned since the 1920s a copy of Erwin Panovsky's pocket selection of Michelangelo drawings published in Germany in 1922.

Michelangelo's 'tremendous monumentality, his over-life-size vision' (in Moore's words to Sylvester) made an equally powerful impression on Bacon, as Martin Harrison demonstrates later in this catalogue; Bacon also placed a high estimate on Michelangelo's drawings. Given the close contact that Sylvester had with both Moore and Bacon at this time – the 1960s – it is difficult not to believe that his conversations with each of them were to a certain extent informed by what the other artist was doing. Although Sylvester's championship of Bacon began later, it was no less comprehensive than his support for Moore, including four editions of published interviews with the painter and the organization of a number of exhibitions of his work. Harrison reminds us that in the early 1970s Bacon talked to Sylvester about wanting to make sculpture, while Sylvester remarked on the increasingly sculptural or plastic quality of Bacon's forms.[37]

interview with Sylvester is spent discussing the Rondanini *Pietà*, which Moore, who had first seen the original in Italy in 1952, now regarded as 'Michelangelo's greatest work ... partly finished, partly unfinished when he died'. He particularly valued its 'disunity of style' (fig.19):

Here again it's ... a contrast between two opposites, like the rough and the smooth, the old and the new, the spiritual and the anatomic. Here in this *Pietà* is the thin expressionist work set against the realistic style of the arm. Why should that hand, which scarcely exists, be so expressive? Why should Michelangelo, out of nothing, achieve that feeling of somebody touching another body with such tenderness? ... It seems to me to have something of the same quality as the late *Crucifixion* drawings ...

Fig.20 | Moore photographing his cast of Auguste Rodin's *Walking Man* 1877–8, Perry Green, 1967

Fig.21 | One of Moore's photographs of the torso of *Walking Man*

Moore and Bacon were further united in their mutual enthusiasm for two great late-nine-teenth-century artists of the human body in motion, Degas and Rodin. In the case of Rodin, Moore came fully to appreciate the French sculptor only after his lengthy absorption in Michelangelo's work; in fact, the two are often interrelated in Moore's mind. As the art historian Albert Elsen has written, 'For him [Moore] no sculptor past or present more than Rodin has so understood the possibilities of treating the figure that were opened up by Michelangelo'.[38] As Moore explained in an interview with Elsen in *Studio International* in 1967:

Rodin taught me a lot about the body; its asymmetry from every point of view; how to avoid rigid symmetry; where were the flexible parts of the body such as those in the head, neck, thorax, pelvis, knees and so on, and that these axes should not parallel each other. These are ways of giving the figure vitality. Rodin perfectly understood Michelangelo.[39]

Working increasingly in bronze from the 1950s, Moore later told Alan Bowness: 'I began to realize that a lot of things one might be using and being influenced by are, compared with Rodin, altogether too easy … As time has gone on, my admiration for Rodin has grown and grown'.[40] Among various aspects of Rodin's sculpture and working practices that he admired, Moore was perhaps most impressed by the compactness and tension in Rodin's figures: the sense of pressure from within, of muscle and bone pushing through to the surface – sculpting from the inside out. He owned a handful of works by Rodin, including a bronze cast of his headless and armless *Walking Man*, 1877–8 (fig.20).[41] Moore photographed the sculpture from numerous angles, fascinated by the effect of light on its richly modelled surface – 'the strongly Michelangelesque quality of concentrated tension, of taut muscles over bone in the upper chest

area', as he put it to Elsen (fig.21). 'I like its springiness, tautness and energy. Every muscle is braced. It all heaves upwards'.[42]

In 1970, at the invitation of the Arts Council, Moore helped to install the Rodin exhibition at the Hayward Gallery (fig.22). A few years later, in 1973, his cast of *Walking Man* was illustrated in the catalogue of the exhibition, *Pioneers of Modern Sculpture*, also held at the Hayward. Elsen, who selected the show and wrote its catalogue, reflected on the significance of *Walking Man* for succeeding generations of sculptors:

Rodin's *Walking Man* … was a sculpture that even Rodin's strongest detractors in the avant-garde could not ignore. Many felt they had to react by remaking it. Rodin had given heroic scale to a partial figure, a non-person. It was his celebration of the life force as well as good modelling …[43]

Another connection between Moore and Bacon was the patronage of the collectors Robert and Lisa Sainsbury. The Sainsburys' support for the two artists early in their careers was decisive and they became friends with both. Moore's *Mother and Child*, 1932, in green Hornton stone, was one of the first works of contemporary art bought by the young Robert Sainsbury in the early 1930s. He and his wife went on to acquire important sculptures and drawings by Moore. They also collected a total of thirteen works by Bacon dating from the 1950s and early 1960s,

including three portraits of Lisa Sainsbury and one of her husband. In April 1959 Robert Sainsbury wrote to Moore: 'Francis Bacon has just finished my portrait. It is a fascinating picture and I am thrilled with it. I hope that when we get back from Greece you will come and see it as well as some of the recent acquisitions.'[44]

In 1978 the 'acquisitions' were opened to the public in the Sainsbury Centre for Visual Arts at the University of East Anglia. There, works by Moore and Bacon sit naturally alongside the Sainsburys' outstanding collection of classical antiquities and tribal art, suggesting affinities across cultures and epochs. Six years earlier, when Robert Sainsbury was a trustee of the Tate Gallery, he and its director Norman Reid flew to Florence for the opening (by Princess Margaret) of Moore's open-air retrospective at the Forte di Belvedere. In a brief letter to Moore written immediately after the May 1972 Tate board meeting, Sainsbury conveyed 'their very best wishes on this rather special occasion' from his fellow trustees: 'We all know how much it means to you in your admiration of Michelangelo and how much it means to other people in their admiration of you.'[45]

Fig.23 | Francis Bacon and Reinhard Hassert
discussing Rodin's *La Terre*, Musée Rodin, Paris, July 1986,
photographed by Eddy Batache

Martin Harrison

BACON AND SCULPTURE

When Francis Bacon 'daydreamed' of ideas for paintings the essence of the image in his imagination – the human body – was, I shall propose, metaphorically three-dimensional – that is, sculptural. Of course, not all of Bacon's paintings respond unproblematically to being considered in terms of their sculptural characteristics: the shallow space in his large 'subject' paintings, in which the image/ground relationship is not always reconciled, is a complicating factor; and his manipulation of 'paint-as-sensation' remained crucial to the realization of the 'image'. But, to invoke Michelangelo at the outset, Bacon's name could be substituted for that of the Renaissance master in John Addington Symonds's succinct phrase: 'Michelangelo's style of design is that of a sculptor ...'.[1] Furthermore, Bacon appears to acknowledge the decisive impact that sculpture made on him in statements such as, 'I would like to make the portraits more sculptural', and 'I think that perhaps the greatest images man has so far made have been in sculpture'.[2]

Among the approximately six hundred extant paintings by Bacon, a handful could logically be described as landscapes (these were painted intermittently), a few are of animal subjects and there are about a hundred small head-and-shoulders portraits. His principal subject, though, was the human figure, or occasionally two figures, set in a confined space. Two main criteria governed the selection of Bacon's paintings for this exhibition: the first was that they shared Henry Moore's iconographical focus on the human head, or standing, seated or lying figures; the other that they should relate, generically or specifically, to sculptural forms.

Many of Bacon's paintings attest to a dialogue with sculpture. It was evinced in the plasticity of his figures, their monumental presentation (the dais, the rail, the pedestal) and to some extent in the way they occupy space. Bacon began to paint in about 1929, but eventually rejected everything he produced during the subsequent fifteen years. It is significant, therefore, that in the painting he came to regard as his 'Opus 1', *Three Studies for Figures at the Base of a Crucifixion*, 1944 (fig.24), the Furies were the most sculptural forms he had painted up to that point. In the early 1950s his Sphinx paintings (fig.25) (he had visited Cairo in 1951) and a series of heads after a life-mask of William Blake depict actual sculptural objects. In addition, he persisted in situating sculptures in the foregrounds of his large paintings, for example in *Reclining Man with Sculpture*, 1960–1 (fig.26), *Portrait of George Dyer and Lucian Freud*, 1967, and *Two Studies of George Dyer with Dog*, 1968.

In an interview with Bacon conducted in 1971, David Sylvester turned to a recurrent topic in their conversations: '... those sculptures you used to talk about wanting to do'.[3] Yet it transpired that Bacon had decided once again not to make sculpture:

I don't think I will do them, because I think I have now found a way by which I could do the images I thought of more satisfactorily in paint than I could in sculpture. I haven't started on them yet, but through thinking of them as sculptures it suddenly came to me how I could make them in paint, and do them much better in paint.[4]

This vacillating between the two media, even if Bacon's motives were different, echoes the famous *paragone* debates in the Italian High Renaissance. These were triggered by Leonardo da Vinci's treatise in which he posited the superiority of painting, against which Michelangelo, albeit with reluctance and exasperatedly, lodged a counter-claim arguing for the supremacy of sculpture.

On another occasion Bacon described in detail his intentions for a sculpturally inflected painting: 'It would be a kind of structured painting in which images, as it were, would arise from a river of flesh. It sounds a terribly romantic idea, but I see it very formally'. He envisaged:

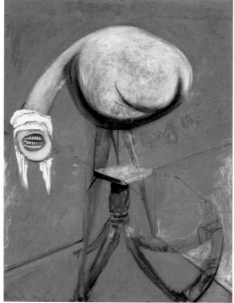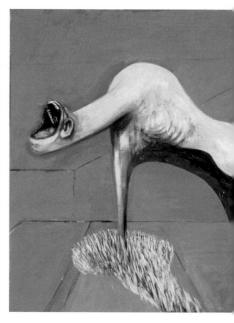

several figures ... raised on structures ... and there would probably be a pavement raised high out of its naturalistic setting, out of which they could move as though out of pools of flesh rose the images, if possible, of people walking on their daily round. I hope to be able to do figures arising out of their own flesh with their bowler hats and umbrellas and make them figures as poignant as a Crucifixion.[5]

He reiterated a related idea in 1974: 'I have decided to make a series of paintings of the sculptures in my mind and see how they come out as paintings', but this time he added, 'And then I might actually start on sculpture.'[6] Furthermore, he was explicit about how he would formulate the sculptures:

I've thought about sculptures on a kind of armature, a very large armature made so that the sculpture could slide along it and people could even alter the position of the sculpture as they wanted. The armature would not be as important as the image, but it would be there to set it off, as I have very often used an armature to set off the image in paintings.[7]

In the event, none of his ideas for sculpture ever materialized. But he had been precise that the figures should be cast in very thin bronze: '... and I've wanted to throw over them a coat of flesh-coloured whitewash ... with the sort of texture of sand and lime that you get'.[8] Ironically, this 'patination' would have returned his sculpture nearer to the condition of painting, like a mixed media '*Tinted Mars*'. The rail (armature) would have been in 'very highly-polished

steel and ... could be slotted so that the image could be screwed into place in different positions'.[9] He envisaged the work on a vast scale: 'I've seen the armature as a very large space, like a street, and the images as comparatively small in relation to the street.'[10] Curiously, nine years later Bacon made a painting, *Statue and Figures in a Street*, 1983 (fig.27), in which several of the constituents correspond with the sculpture he had planned. Bacon's friend, the photographer Peter Beard, arranged an exhibition of Bacon's sculptures with the dealer and curator Irving Blum in New York, and the project proceeded as far as researching flesh-coloured and clear plastics that would have been used to represent the Eumenides on a rail; the project foundered when, in Beard's words 'it was voted down by abstract expressionist artists'.[11]

Painting and Sculpture

Asked about how the ideas for his paintings were generated, Bacon said that 'I can daydream for hours and pictures fall in just like slides'.[12] While the claim to such fecundity might need to be treated with scepticism, he also implied that he was a receiver of images, which interestingly he expressed as a 'photographic' metaphor.[13] But how does any artist approach the blank canvas? Like Bacon, Caravaggio, for example, notwithstanding the vaunted naturalism that causes his paintings to resonate so powerfully, did not employ preliminary drawings in the conventional sense of detailed preparatory studies. It could be argued that Caravaggio's representation of, say,

Fig.24 | Francis Bacon, *Three Studies for Figures at the Base of a Crucifixion*, 1944, Tate, London

Fig.25 | Francis Bacon, *Sphinx III*, 1954, Hirshhorn Museum and Sculpture Garden, Washington DC

Fig.26 | Francis Bacon, *Reclining Man with Sculpture*, 1960–61, Museum of Contemporary Art, Tehran

Fig.27 | Francis Bacon, *Statue with Figures in Street*, 1983, Private Collection

the *Death of the Virgin*, c.1601–6 (Louvre Museum), was prescribed by the requirements of his patron, the conventions of Counter-Reformation iconography and by its architectural function as an altarpiece.[14] Yet in mood, intensity of expression and the disposition of dramatically illuminated figures in space, the *Death of the Virgin* was virtually without precedent. It is unlikely that Caravaggio embarked on such an imposing picture without having envisaged the key elements of the composition beforehand, and his *alla prima* method still necessitated the laying down of the principal contours of his paintings, a technique confirmed by x-ray investigations which have revealed both under-drawing and incisions.

Since Bacon, too, was not an automatist, he must have had an idea about the painting he was about to make. His holograph notes of ideas for paintings are written equivalents of drawings, and what might properly be called preparatory were the

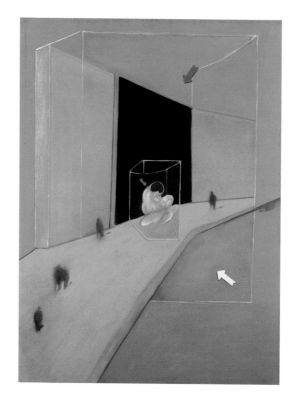

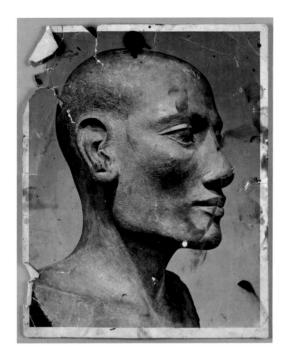

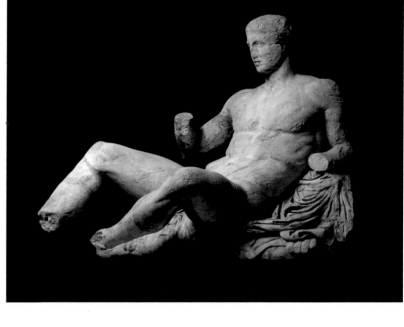

broad outlines of a composition that Bacon roughly sketched out in thinned oils; the surviving canvases that were abandoned at this early stage suggest, on the other hand, that these initial applications were sometimes fairly exploratory. Gilles Deleuze defined Bacon's process in terms of the first and second stages of figuration, whereby the second stage neutralizes the primary figuration in a move to eliminate the figurative or a narrative. Norman Bryson described a painter's procedures with this nuance: 'a first image is placed on the canvas in order to induce in the painter a reaction that will replace it';[15] the second image generates a third, and so on, each stage ruthlessly effacing its predecessors in a process of erasure that only ceases 'when the initial image is completely subverted'.[16] Into Bryson's deictic account one could insert the accidents, the unforeseeable consequences of 'splashing the stuff down' that for Bacon was the crucial determining role of chance in his paintings, distancing them from a straightforward narrative while not entirely eliminating it.

Evidently Bacon felt no obligation to be consistent in his remarks on the art of the past: he was, after all, an artist not an art historian. He plundered great art with an acute intelligence: not solely iconoclastically, he dismantled the Grand Manner through the modern medium of photography. But among the 'greatest images' he once cited 'some of the great Egyptian sculpture, of course, and Greek sculpture too' (fig.28).[17] The resonance of Greek sculpture was doubtless intensified by Bacon's awareness of the surrealist trope of the body-in-pieces, reinforced by his familiarity with the writings of Georges Bataille on fragmentation in the broader philosophical sense. He was intimately acquainted with Greek and Roman prototypes such as the Belvedere Torso, and regularly visited the British Museum to see the Elgin Marbles (fig.29), which 'are always very important to me';[18] significantly, however, he pondered whether their effect on him was more profound 'because they're fragments, and whether if one had seen the whole images they would seem as poignant as they seem as fragments'.[19]

Bacon also connected the poignancy of fragmentation to Michelangelo, of whom he said: 'I've always thought about Michelangelo; he's always been deeply important in my way of thinking about form.'[20] Despite Michelangelo's enduring effect on his oeuvre, Bacon remarked: 'although I have this profound admiration for all his work, the work I like most is the drawings. For me he is one of the greatest draughtsmen, if not the greatest' (fig.30).[21] 'As most of my figures are taken from the male nude', Bacon added, 'I am sure that I have been influenced by the fact that Michelangelo made the most voluptuous nudes …'.[22]

Next to Picasso, Michelangelo was the artist that Bacon most assiduously consulted. He was highly selective in his Picasso enthusiasms, but it was the most sculptural of his paintings – *Les Demoiselles*

Fig.28 | 'Salt Head', leaf torn by Bacon from C.D. Noblecourt, *The Sculpture of Ancient Egypt*, 1960, Dublin City Gallery, The Hugh Lane

Fig.29 | Figure of Dionysos, from the east pediment of the Parthenon, c.438–432 BC, British Museum, London

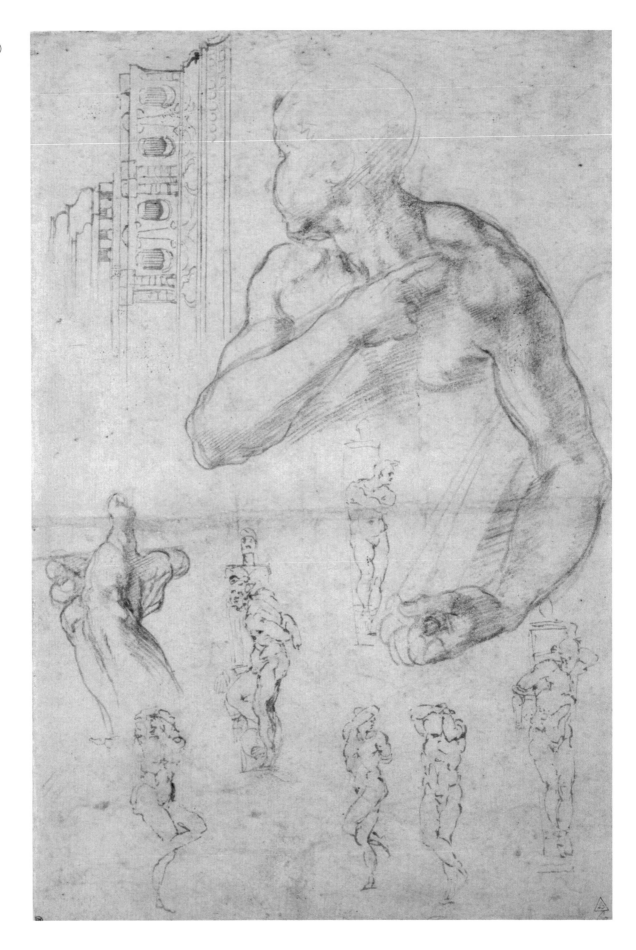

Fig.30 | Michelangelo
Buanarroti (1475–1564)
*Studies for the Sistine
Ceiling and the Tomb of
Pope Julius II* c.1508–12
Ashmolean Museum,
University of Oxford

Fig.31 | Francis Bacon, *Triptych – Studies of the Human Body*, 1979, Private Collection. (left panel)

Fig.32 | Michelangelo Buonarotti, *Study for the figure of 'Day' (Medici chapel)*, c.1520–23, Ashmolean Museum, University of Oxford

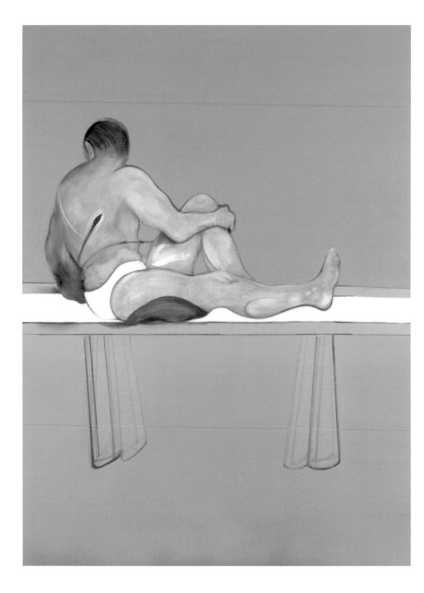

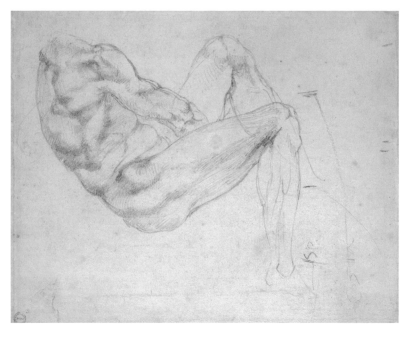

d'Avignon, 1907, and the beachscapes inspired by Marie-Thérèse Walter – that had the profoundest effect on his paintings. As we shall see, Michelangelo's example informed Bacon's paintings in various ways. The reclining figures of George Dyer in the central and right-hand panels of *Three Figures in a Room*, 1964, were freely based on *Evening* and *Dawn*, c.1524–34, on the sarcophagus of Lorenzo in the Medici Chapel, Florence. In *Triptych: Studies of the Human Body*, 1979 (fig.31), the seated figures in the outer panels are similarly indebted to the figure representing *Day*, c.1526–34, on the tomb of Giuliano (fig.32), albeit the source image is substantially modified. In neither painting, however, was Bacon aiming to evoke the quintessential Michelangelo, although the elevated art-historical sanction doubtless appealed to him; instead he selected details to appropriate that were germane to his own paintings. It is plausible that Bacon's partial, oblique quotations occurred particularly when he worked from photographs but was unfamiliar with the originals: as he said of the Medici tombs, 'I think they're absolutely astonishing, but I haven't actually seen them.'[23]

The gestural language that Bacon deployed for his male nudes was based partly on Eadweard Muybridge's sequential photographs of the human figure in motion, but ultimately evolved from a complex trialogue between himself, Muybridge and Michelangelo. The heterogeneity and multiplicity of Bacon's absorptions is demonstrated in *Two Studies from the Human Body*, 1975 (cat.60). The principal figure in motion probably borrows from Muybridge's serial photographs of a man throwing a discus, but Bacon's quoting of pictorial sources was seldom this straightforward and he may also have had in mind a classical discobolus (he was certainly familiar with the casts in the British Museum and the Terme Museum in Rome, fig.33), as well as the pendulous arm in Rodin's bronze, *La Grande Ombre*, 1880 (fig.34).

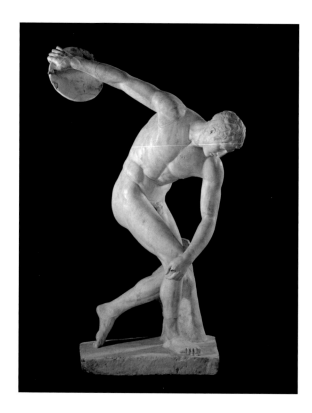

Fig.33 | Discobolus, (Roman copy of a bronze original, 5th century BC), British Museum, London

Fig.34 | Auguste Rodin, *La Grande Ombre*. As reproduced in Jean Charbonneaux, *Les Sculptures de Rodin*, Paris, 1949; Bacon owned a copy of this book.

Fig.35 | Michelangelo Buonarotti, *'Young Slave'*, c.1516–19, Victoria & Albert Museum, London

Bacon tended to avoid being specific about his inspirations, except when they were so obvious that to affect ignorance of them would have been fatuous. But in elucidating his preference for his paintings to be framed under glass he remarked: 'If you go into the Victoria and Albert Museum there's a wax figure of Michelangelo [sic] which is in a glass case. Well, it's very much more beautiful in the glass case than if it were in the open. It's more beautiful because it's been removed further from you.'[24] He was referring to the small wax model of a *Young Slave*, c.1516–19, a design for the tomb of Pope Julius II (fig.35).[25] The modello must have been well known to Bacon, whose uncle, Sir Cecil Harcourt-Smith, had been the Director of the Victoria and Albert Museum from 1909 to 1924; for most of his adult life Bacon seldom lived more than a few minutes distance from the Museum, and visited it frequently.

The diminutive but potent wax figure almost certainly acted as a stimulus for the figure in one of Bacon's most enigmatic works, *Painting*, 1950 (fig.36), which is formally unique in his output. He also owned many books with reproductions of Michelangelo's drawings, and so would have been familiar with the original of the *Dying Slave* in the Louvre Museum (fig.37). It is not insignificant, in this context, that the two twentieth-century masters whom Bacon most revered, Picasso and Matisse, both owned plaster casts of the *Dying Slave*. But the proximity in London of the wax model places it strongly in contention as having informed the figure in *Painting*.

It is a paradox of Bacon's art that while he made paintings with undiluted forthrightness, and was ostensibly unconcerned with their reception, he simultaneously deflected the gaze – the equivalent visceral response of the viewer – by virtue of the reflections that occur on the screens of glass that he insisted should protect his paintings, removing them 'further from you'. Bacon was one of the most contradictory of artists, and we encounter here the

Portraits and Sculpture

dichotomy of his Eros and Thanatos drives, which was paramount in so many of his paintings. The anti-psychologistic stance of many recent art theorists has discouraged this kind of analysis, and Bacon was adept at deflecting questions about his subconscious. Yet as early as 1949 he had explained to a journalist, 'Painting is the pattern of one's own nervous system being projected on the canvas'.[26]

Bacon's paintings are troubling, but they abundantly repay prolonged scrutiny and contemplation. One of the most influential writers on Bacon, Gilles Deleuze, denied that Bacon's paintings were representational, or that they embodied narrative or autobiographical connotations: the present writer insists on the relevance of their iconography. Bacon claimed that his paintings were saying nothing, but invariably he painted people, or subjects, that were of consequence to him – a lover or a friend, violence, sex or death. About *Lying Figure in a Mirror*, 1971 (cat.59), for example, of which there is a preliminary discussion here (p.138), Deleuze only remarks, 'it counts as two Figures, it is a veritable diagram of sensation',[27] which is so reductive as to say next to nothing.

Bacon's ostensible indifference to the opinions of viewers, critics or buyers of his paintings is, nevertheless, legendary. One prominent collector, the owner of ten major Bacons, told me that when Bacon was a dinner guest at his house in the 1970s he resolutely refused to even glance at his paintings; instead, he advised his host, who also possessed one of Matisse's early sculptured heads of *Jeanette*, 1916, that he should buy the other four heads that Matisse made of *Jeanette* in preference to more of his own paintings. Other Bacon collectors have explained how he would never waver, under any pressure or circumstance, from declining outright to discuss the meaning of his paintings.

Most of Bacon's paintings from 1950 onwards could be categorized as portraits. Regardless of how extreme or implausible the situation in which he placed his subjects, he almost invariably had an individual in mind. Yet, ironically, the first painting in which an individual was named in the title, *Portrait of Lucian Freud*, 1951, was a full-length representation in which Freud's pose was copied from a photograph of Franz Kafka with his sister and the resemblance to Freud (although Freud thought otherwise) is unconvincing; Freud related that when he arrived to sit for Bacon, 'he found the portrait almost completely finished'.[28] If Bacon was dissatisfied with the individuation in this painting it may have pushed him towards the new strategies for achieving a convincing likeness that he was soon employing with conviction. Initially this entailed similitude of the head within a full-length portrait, but what became his standardized format for head-and-shoulders portraits, 35.5 × 30.5 cm (14 × 12 in), was established in about 1959.

Significantly, the precursors of this new portrait format were all inspired by sculpture. For the three portraits he made of Lisa Sainsbury she sat to him many times, yet *Sketch for a Portrait of Lisa*, 1955 (fig.38), appears to reference mainly Egyptian sculpture, although it is also the closest Bacon came to a Fayum mummy portrait. Its direct pictorial source was probably the same as that for the painting *Head*, 1956, which was based on a photograph of King Akhenaten in Kurt Lange's book, *König Echnaton und die Amarna-zeit* (1951; fig.39). Before embarking on the portraits of Lisa Sainsbury, however, Bacon had made four paintings 'After the Life-mask of William Blake' (fig.40, cat.49). The subject was prompted by the composer Gerard Schurmann having asked Bacon in 1954 to provide a cover illustration for the score

Fig.38 | Francis Bacon, *Sketch for a Portrait of Lisa*, 1955, Sainsbury Centre for Visual Arts, UEA, Norwich

Fig.39 | King Akhenaten. As reproduced in Kurt Lange, *König Echnaton und die Amarna-Zeit*, 1951; Bacon owned a copy of this book.

Fig.40 | Francis Bacon, *Study for Portrait III (After the life-mask of William Blake)*, 1955, Private Collection (cat.49)

Fig.41 | Photograph of James Deville's life-mask of William Blake, 1823, National Portrait Gallery, London

of his *Nine Poems of William Blake*. Schurmann and Bacon went together to the National Portrait Gallery, London, to view James S. Deville's life-mask of Blake (1823). Although the original was three-dimensional Bacon painted the whole series from black-and-white photographs (fig.41). Much later, Lawrence Gowing made a gift to Bacon of a plaster cast of the Blake head, which appears in several photographs of Bacon's Reece Mews studio. Its presence there, however, was posterior to the paintings, and Gowing admitted that his attempt to persuade Bacon to paint from the actual object had not only failed, but had also been misguided.

From 1961 onwards Bacon's small head-and shoulders portraits constituted a significant proportion of his oeuvre. Although to achieve a degree of verisimilitude in these paintings Bacon made use of photographs, the 'sources' were almost entirely abandoned during his performances in paint, in the distortions and the surging intensity of flesh rendered in pigment. Many of Bacon's friends have recounted how, under the artist's intense, prolonged gaze, they felt like a 'moth on a pin',[29] and this close scrutiny was transposed into his urgent, visceral portraits. Michael Andrews, who entered the Slade School of Art in 1949, just as Bacon was coming to prominence in London,

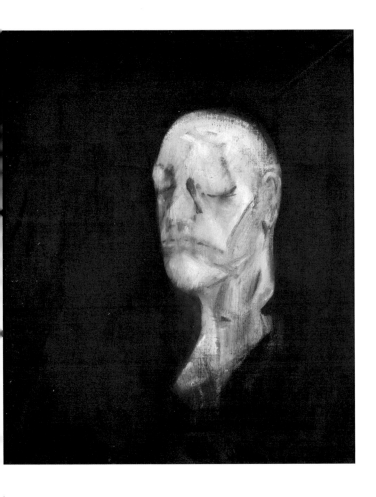
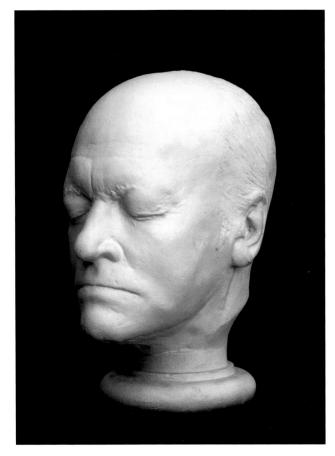

recalled how 'at the time we found [Bacon's] ideas very intoxicating, like the idea of a single tragic figure … No matter how they were done they still lit up and made exciting the business of looking at, of staring at, of appraising someone for a long time.'[30]

In a now-familiar meeting with the artist Brian Wall that took place in St Ives, Cornwall, in 1959, Bacon, pretending not to know the answer, asked Wall what he did. 'I'm a sculptor', replied Wall; 'How interesting', Bacon retorted, 'actually there are only three: Michelangelo, Rodin and Brancusi.'[31] Bacon's insensitive retort was doubtless intended to provoke, but it also serves to confirm his admiration for the

three sculptors he cited. The studio that Bacon rented in St Ives was shared by Peter Lanyon and one of the port's few figurative artists, William Redgrave, and they ran it as an art school, St Peter's Loft. In the year before Bacon's visit, Wall had embarked on what were the first abstract welded-steel sculptures made in Britain; since Bacon no doubt found these forms uncongenial, it was perhaps partly in reaction to them that he encouraged Redgrave in his experiments with sculpture. The first portrait sculpture that Redgrave made was a lively bust of Bacon that was admired by Bacon himself, as well as Sir John Rothenstein and Sir Robert Sainsbury (fig.42).

Significantly, Bacon's rebuff of Wall was uttered at the precise moment at which Rodin's sculpture most decisively informed his paintings. Since 1950 Bacon had represented a majority of his figures in static poses. Many of them were seated (the Popes, the Man in Blue series), and their monumentality reflected Bacon's admiration for Egyptian sculpture as much as, in the case of the Popes, the Velázquez prototype. In his 1956–7 variations of Van Gogh's self-portrait in the *Painter on the Road to Tarascon* of 1888, Bacon had pushed himself to rethink the question of the mobile human body in space, an exercise that may have initiated the expansion of his repertory of articulated postures demonstrated in *Lying Figure*, 1959 (cat.50), and the reclining and lying figures that succeeded it. He drew on a wide range of visual stimuli in order to accomplish this, some of it in reproduction rather than at first hand. It included Degas' monotypes, thirty-six of which had been exhibited at the Lefevre Gallery, London, in Spring 1958, together with five Degas bronzes, in addition to Gauguin's Pont-Aven paintings and Soutine's portraits, while Muybridge and Michelangelo were ever-present in this interplay of imagery.

For the radical exaggerations and distortions that Bacon was about to introduce, Rodin's sculptures were paramount. Their outstretched limbs, fractured forms and articulation of transitional movement were catalysts for the transformation in Bacon's art, manifested in all the paintings of lying, reclining and sleeping figures that Bacon painted between 1959 and 1961. Rodin's sculptures were accessible to Bacon in a way that the Medici Chapel tombs were not, for he never visited Florence (fig.43). While Bacon had innumerable photographs of the work of both artists at his disposal, experiencing Rodin's sculpture in the round, its 'unfinishedness' and surface textures, literally brought another dimension to the encounter. In addition to the eighteen sculptures that Rodin had presented to

Fig.43 | Rodin's installation of his sculptures at the Victoria & Albert Museum, London

Fig.44 | Auguste Rodin, *Iris Messenger of the Gods*. As reproduced in Jean Charbonneaux, *Les Sculptures de Rodin*, Paris, 1949; Bacon owned a copy of this book.

the Victoria and Albert Museum in 1914 (including *Iris, Messenger of the Gods* and *Crouching Woman*), the Tate Gallery acquired seven Rodin sculptures between 1925 and 1960, among which Bacon is likely to have responded to works such as the bronze head of *Balzac*, 1892. *Balzac* was donated by Sir Michael Sadler in 1931, two years before he became Bacon's first patron, other than family or friends; Sadler had also bought Henry Moore's work by this time, and by 1936 he owned at least ten carvings and two drawings by Moore.

In Bacon's lying and reclining figures, the splayed limbs and exposed genitals are particularly redolent of three of Rodin's bronzes, all made about 1890–91: *Crouching Woman*, *Flying Figure* and *Iris, Messenger of the Gods* (fig.44). Since Bacon was reluctant to discuss his pictorial sources, identifying his inspirations is often necessarily conjectural, although his studio contents, now deposited in Dublin City Gallery The Hugh Lane, are proving to be a fertile resource in this respect, removing the need for some of the speculation. But the chance survival of a memorandum, never of course intended for public consumption, afforded a rare opportunity to be conclusive about Rodin: one of the copies Bacon owned of V.J. Stanek's *Introducing Monkeys* (1957) is annotated on a flyleaf: 'use figure volante of Rodin on sofa arms raised'; on the same page he also inscribed: 'Figure as Rodin figure on sofa in centre of room with arms raised'. His friend Eddy Batache, who frequently visited the Musée Rodin with Bacon in the 1970s and 1980s, has confirmed Bacon's continuing interest in Rodin, and his close scrutiny of, for example, not only *Iris* but also the equally fractured *La Terre*, 1894.

Flying Figure was presented by Rodin as an autonomous fragment – a female torso severed from the figures of *Avarice* and *Lust* in the 'Gates of Hell'. Rodin especially, and Bacon at a remove, had to meet the challenge of the master, and no doubt Rainer

Fig.45 | Francis Bacon, *Study of the Human Body – from a Drawing by Ingres*, 1982, Hirshhorn Museum and Sculpture Garden, Washington DC.(right panel of *Diptych 1982–84*)

Fig.46 | Auguste Rodin, *Man with a Broken Nose*. As reproduced in Jean Charbonneaux, *Les Sculptures de Rodin*, Paris, 1949; Bacon owned a copy of this book.

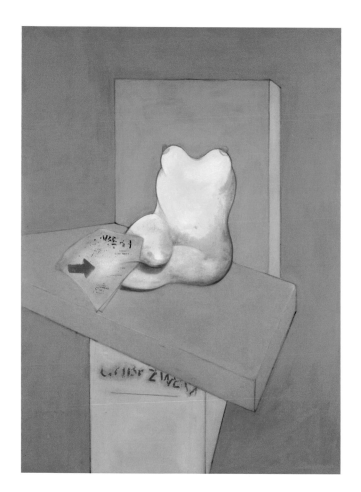

Maria Rilke's description of Rodin's perception of Michelangelo adumbrates Bacon's response: 'All his statues are so constrained by agony that they seem to wish to break themselves. They all seem ready to succumb to the pressure of despair which fills them. When Michelangelo was old, he actually broke them. Art did not content him. He wanted infinity.'[32] Abruptly truncated forms, reworked from Ingres' Sphinxes and the women in *Le Bain Turc*, 1862, featured prominently in Bacon's later paintings, for example *Study of the Human Body – from a Drawing by Ingres*, 1982, (Hirshhorn Museum and Sculpture Garden, Washington DC) (fig.45), in which a mutilated torso terminates in a pair of breasts, and the similarly anatomically abbreviated *Untitled (Kneeling Figure)*, of around 1982 (cat.62).

If the disposition of the limbs in Rodin's sculpture critically informed Bacon's reconfigurations of the human body, scarcely less significant was the impact of his dynamic, tactile surfaces, although as a painter Bacon had to convey motion as a different type of illusion on a two-dimensional canvas. Bacon alluded to this phenomenon in his encomium for Géricault, who 'somehow had movement pinned to the body'.[33] The most direct analogy in Bacon's paintings – and this can only be observed satisfactorily in their presence – is visible in the movement and vigour of the brushstrokes. According to Ronald Alley and Lucian Freud, Bacon's *Head of a Man*, 1959, was painted from life, which may have been a factor in the realism and immediacy of the portrayal. The vitality of its rapid, broad brushwork and dabbed textures again recalls Rodin's powerful bronze heads, particularly the mobile surfaces of *Man with Broken Nose*, the *Iris*; *Large Head* (a version of the head of *Crouching Woman*) and the head of *Balzac.Head of a Man* resembles an accelerated recapitulation of *Man with Broken Nose* (fig.46) as described in Rilke's paean to Rodin's modus operandi:

There is on this head no line, no exaggeration, no contour that Rodin has not seen and willed ... One knows that some of the marks on this face were engraved slowly, hesitatingly, that others were traced gently and afterwards drawn in strongly by some habit or thought that came again and again ...[34]

In his turning figures of 1962 and 1963 Bacon continued to extend Rodin's paradigms of the body-in-motion, briefly experimenting with a heightened contrapposto in *Figure Turning*, 1962, in which one foot is lifted from the ground and the head is turned through ninety degrees. This was one of four important and closely related paintings made in Spring 1962, another of which, *Seated Figure*, 1962 (cat.55), reprises elements of *Study from Innocent X*, 1962, which had been completed two months earlier, laterally reversing the restless Pope and stripping the representation to a more elemental 'man'.

The contemporaneous *Three Studies for a Crucifixion*, 1962 (Solomon R. Guggenheim Museum, New York) is frequently regarded as a pivotal work, signalling a 'return to form' in the opinions of critics who had regarded Bacon's output in the years since 1957 as representing a decline. Clearly intended by Bacon as a consummatory flourish for his first major retrospective at the Tate Gallery, its imagery harks back to the breakthrough *Three Studies for Figures at the Base of a Crucifixion* triptych of 1944. The black biomorph lurching into the corner of the right-hand panel relates to the recurrent Bacon motif of death shadowing life, or again to Eros and Thanatos. Its form is redolent of the black sheep in Gauguin's *Le Christ Vert*, 1889, and Max Ernst's bird heads, such as *Bonjour Satanas*, 1928. The connection should only be regarded as speculative, but the head of the biomorph is also comparable with Henry Moore's *Mother and Child*, 1936. Bacon's interest in Moore, especially in the 1930s and 1940s, should not be underestimated,

notwithstanding his dismissive comments on the shelter drawings. *Mother and Child* was bought in 1937 by Roland Penrose, who upset his conservative neighbours when he erected it in the front garden of his house in Hampstead; by 1962 he had moved the sculpture to his country house in Sussex, and thus Bacon, who visited the Penroses there, had ample opportunity to see it.

The triptych *Three Studies of the Male Back*, 1970, was inspired, Bacon told Hugh Davies, by 'a paratrooper staying here who was a magnificent specimen', but he admitted that Matisse's four large bronze reliefs, *Nu de Dos I–IV*, c.1909–30, which had been purchased by the Tate Gallery in 1958, 'might have affected him'.[35] Given Bacon's obvious fascination with Matisse, it is puzzling that he opted to play it down so persistently, comparing Matisse unfavourably with Picasso, for example, because he lacked the Spanish artist's 'brutality of fact'. Matisse's *Reclining Nude II*, 1927 (fig.47), had entered the Tate collection in 1953, and together with Matisse's many variants of the bronze reclining figure, as well as drawings and paintings of odalisques, it was doubtless among the wide range of imagery that informed Bacon's *Lying Figure in a Mirror*, 1971 (cat.59). In this respect Michelangelo's allegorical (female) figure of *Night*, 1526–31, in the Medici Chapel was of equal importance to both Matisse and Bacon.

Bacon's interest in sculpture never dimmed. He profoundly admired Giacometti's drawings, but professed to be indifferent to his sculpture, although *Palace at 4 a.m.*, 1932, might well have affected his internal cage structures, or 'space-frames'. From the late 1960s he was close to the 'Pop' sculptor Clive Barker, whose life-masks of Bacon were exhibited together with Bacon's diptych portrait of Barker at the Felicity Samuel Gallery in 1978; Bacon's untypical *Water Running from a Tap*, 1982 (fig.48), appears to be a response to Barker's *Splash*, 1967 (fig.49). He was

Fig.47 | Henri Matisse, *Reclining Nude II*, 1927, Tate, London

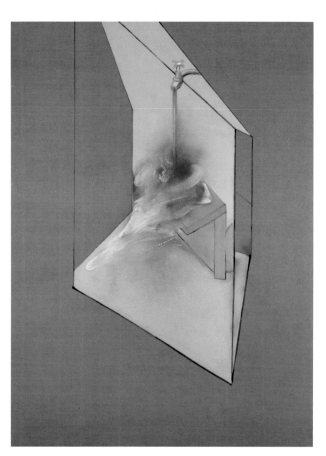

Fig.48 | Francis Bacon, *Water from a Running Tap*, 1982, Private Collection

Fig.49 | Clive Barker, *Splash*, 1967, Tate, London

friendly, too, with the Boyle family, and a sincere admirer of their Earth Pieces and Body Works.

Bacon's last major painting, *Triptych*, 1991, perpetuated the referencing of sculpture, not only in the abbreviated figures themselves but in the funereal black slabs that frame them in each panel; he had employed this device, reminiscent of headstones on monuments or the portals of Egyptian tombs, since *Triptych August 1972*, a memorial to George Dyer. David Sylvester remarked to an artist friend that the centre panel of *Triptych*, 1991 (fig.50), with the coupling males (a pared-down development of the Muybridge photographs of wrestlers that Bacon had first used thirty-eight years previously), was 'one of his favourite late Henry Moores'.[36] While this was a playful comment, made by a critic who had been close to both men, it was not merely flippant. As Grey Gowrie noted, 'Bacon is an artist of endgame. His work is a lifespan distant from Moore's family groups or mothers-with-child',[37] yet for all their manifest differences Bacon and Moore were two great artists striving to represent the human condition in the atomic age.

Fig.50 | Francis Bacon, *Triptych* 1991, Museum of Modern Art, New York. (centre panel)

BACON
MOORE

Early Sculpture

Moore's early sculptures are mainly carvings in stone or wood, informed by the doctrine of 'truth to material' then fashionable among the avant-garde. 'Every material has its own individual qualities', he wrote in 1934.

It is only when the sculptor works direct, when there is an active relationship with his material, that the material can take its part in the shaping of an idea. Stone, for example, is hard and concentrated and should not be falsified to look like flesh ... It should keep its hard tense stoniness.[1]

At this date Moore drew inspiration from non-European cultures, especially pre-Colombian art. *Mask*, 1929 (cat.1), resembles the Mezcala mask from Mexico which he owned. Moore had noticed that Mexican masks were often asymmetrical: 'one eye is quite different from the other, and the mouth is at an angle bringing back the balance'.[2] He later remarked that 'everybody's face ... is asymmetrical'.[3] From 1930 Moore's sculptures show the influence of the biomorphic forms in Picasso's work of the late 1920s. Even though the half-human, half-animal female figures of 1931, both entitled *Composition* (cats 2 and 3), were carved – one in stone, the other in alabaster – they have a sensuous, organic feel suggestive of flesh. In the 1934 *Composition* (cat.4), Moore reduces the human body even further, to a collection of bone-like shapes on a tabletop, echoing Giacometti's surrealist sculptures of the early 1930s. *Three Points*, 1939–40 (cat.5), recalls the open mouths of the terrified horse and crying mother in Picasso's *Guernica*, 1937, although Moore compared the sense of anticipation which he hoped the sculpture would provoke to the charge given off by a spark plug: the points are not quite touching. Moore's interest in the open mouth and menacing tongue is shared by Bacon – for example, in his *Three Studies for Figures at the Base of a Crucifixion*, 1944 (fig.24), or *Head II*, 1949

(cat.46). With both artists the origin was probably the surrealist preoccupation with violence and the erotic. A more specific source may have been Picasso's painting *Abstraction*, 1929, illustrated in Herbert Read's book *Art Now* (1933), which also reproduced Moore's *Composition*, 1931 (cat.3) and Bacon's early *Crucifixion*, 1933 (fig.51).

In 1938–40 Moore made a small number of sculptures in lead, including *The Helmet* (cat.6, later bronze cast). This is the first of Moore's 'opened-out' heads, anticipated in earlier reclining figures, in which void or space is allowed to penetrate solid form and become an equal element in the composition. *The Helmet* is also the first sculpture by Moore in which a smaller form is enclosed by a larger one, suggesting, in this case, maternal protection. The head–armour analogy was very much of its time, as Britain moved inexorably towards war and Moore (who was by now over forty) joined his local Home Guard.

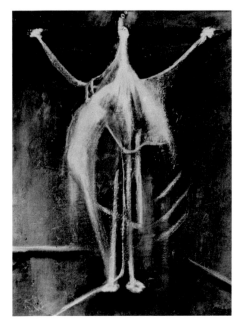

Fig.51 | Francis Bacon, *Crucifixion* 1933 (from Herbert Read, *Art Now*, London 1933).

1 MASK 1929

Cast concrete · H 21.6 cm
Leeds Museums and Galleries
(Leeds Art Gallery)

2 COMPOSITION 1931

Blue Hornton stone · H 48.3 cm
The Henry Moore Family Collection

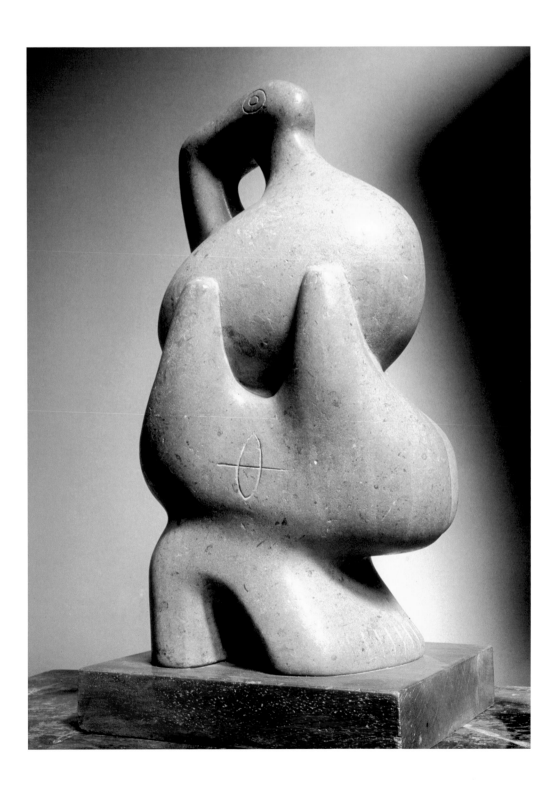

3 COMPOSITION 1931

Cumberland alabaster · L 41.5 cm
The Henry Moore Foundation: gift of Irina Moore, 1979

4 COMPOSITION 1934

Cast concrete · L 44.5 cm
The Henry Moore Foundation: gift of the artist, 1977

5 THREE POINTS 1939–40

Cast iron, unique · L 20.0 cm
The Henry Moore Foundation: gift of Irina Moore, 1977

6 THE HELMET 1939–40

Bronze · H 29.2 cm
Cast: Fiorini, London, 1959
The Henry Moore Foundation: gift of Irina Moore, 1977

Drawings

Initially, drawing was the genesis of all Moore's sculpture. 'In my opinion', he wrote, 'long and intense study of the human figure is the necessary foundation for a sculptor'.[4] His earliest surviving life drawings date from the early 1920s, such as *Standing Nude* (cat.7), which anticipates the static weightiness of his sculpture. From the 1950s Moore would prefer to derive his sculptural ideas from a hand-size model or maquette, which more often than not incorporated a found object such as a bone or flint.

The rest of the drawings grouped in this section were all done during the Second World War. The German bombing provided Moore with a succession of incongruous, often surreal subjects, giving full scope to the metamorphic richness of his imagination. Mouths are transformed into beaked heads, heads into traps or weapons (cat.9), humans become hollowed-out metallic shells filled with mechanical innards (cats 8 and 10), day turns into night, the living appear dying (cat.14). As an official war artist in 1940–1, Moore drew the people sheltering from the Blitz in the London Underground, many with gaping mouths and adopting extreme bodily positions in sleep (cats 11, 12 and 13), which have been compared to the corpses excavated from the ruins of Pompeii.[5] Although these drawings tend to be more naturalistic, they are far from a documentary record of what Moore observed. For example, the mass of anonymous bodies shrouded in blankets evoke Egyptian mummies, while the Tube shelter resembles some vast catacomb. The odour of death clings to many of these images.

Kenneth Clark thought that an 'Aeschylean sense of menace [was] present in all Moore's drawings of the 1940s'.[6] With *Three Fates*, 1941 (cat.15), and related shelter drawings (cat.16) we are certainly in the world of Greek mythology, if not tragedy. Three seated women with monstrous heads – one holding a baby, the second knitting and the third staring into space – evoke the characters of Clotho, Lachesis and Atropos, who are 'usually old and ugly' and 'are generally depicted spinning the thread of life, and measuring and cutting off the allotted length'.[7] Associated with night, sleep and death, they add an element of archetypal drama and psychological depth to Moore's vision of wartime hardship and endurance.

Three Fates introduces the idea of grouping figures into threes, which Moore would later carry over into his sculptural practice. It also relates to Bacon's regular use of the triptych format from 1962 onwards, for which his earlier *Three Studies for Figures at the Base of a Crucifixion*, 1944 (fig.24), is the prototype. Bacon described the grotesque hybrids in this painting as Furies or Eumenides (Aeschylus again), who, as agents of punishment and avengers of wrong, had a similar function to the Fates. *Three Studies* was first shown at the Lefevre Gallery, London, in April 1945, its background of lurid orange echoing some of the fiery colours in Moore's Blitz and shelter drawings. The latter are usually a mixture of water-colour and crayon – presumably the reason they were called 'paintings' when some were included in the same exhibition.

In the Lefevre show, Moore was represented by two 1930s sculptures and fourteen wartime drawings of draped figures, seated figures in claustrophobic and cell-like rooms, family groups and so on (fig.52). Although Moore was well known, this was Bacon's first appearance in public (he had been recommended to the gallery by Graham Sutherland, another of the exhibitors). It was also the first time that Bacon and Moore had exhibited together. Most reviewers were dismissive of Bacon's *Three Studies* but Raymond Mortimer in the *New Statesman* noted that 'these objects are perched on stools, and depicted as if they were sculpture, as in the Picassos of 1930'.[8]

Moore's second commission as part of the War Artists scheme was to make a series of drawings of coalminers (cats 17, 18 and 19). He found it a forma-tive experience which had important implications for his sculpture. 'Through these coalmine drawings, I discovered the male figure and the qualities of the figure in action. As a sculptor, I had previously believed only in static forms, that is, forms in repose.'[9]

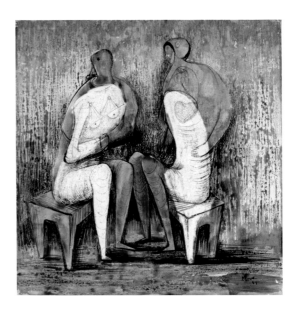

Fig.52 | *Two Seated Figures*, 1944, Private Collection. One of the fourteen drawings Moore exhibited at the Lefevre Gallery in April 1945, in a group show that included Bacon.

7 STANDING NUDE c.1924

Pen and ink, and chalk on paper · 32.3 × 21.4 cm
Inscribed l.l. *Moore*
The Henry Moore Foundation: gift of the artist, 1977

8 SHEET OF STUDIES FOR SCULPTURE 1940

Pencil, chalk, wax crayon, watercolour, pen and ink on paper
25.2 × 43.2 cm
Inscribed l.r. *Moore* / 40; and u.c. *The human body is not solid* [...]
/ *but that is* [...] *more reason for it to be a subject for* / *sculpture, it*
means that the sculptor cannot be a copyist / *but must make changes*
& recreate it; and u.c.r. *The human body is what we know most about,*
because / *its* [sic] *ourselves & so it moves us most strongly*
Ashmolean Museum, University of Oxford: presented by the
Contemporary Art Society, 1944 (WA1944.88)

9 SHEET OF HEADS SHOWING SECTIONS 1940

Wax crayon, coloured crayon, watercolour wash, pen and ink on paper
27.9 × 38.1 cm
Inscribed l.r. *Moore / 40* and u.c. *Sheet of heads showing sections*
The Henry Moore Foundation: acquired 2002

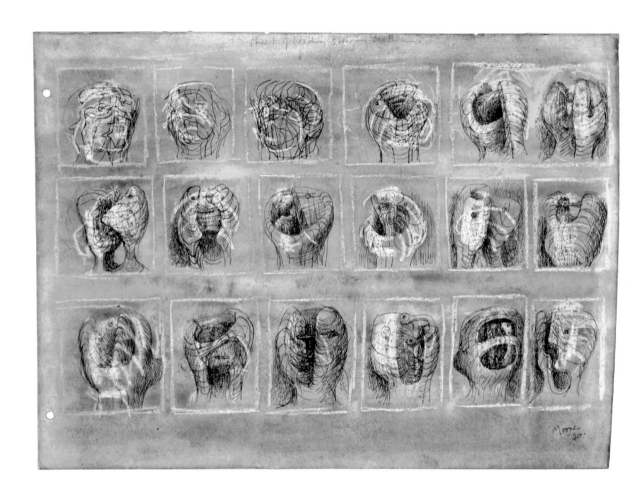

10 TWO STANDING FIGURES 1940

Pencil, wax crayon, coloured crayon, watercolour wash,
pen and ink on paper · 51.5 × 38.7 cm
Inscribed l.r. *Moore / 40*
Ashmolean Museum, University of Oxford: presented by
Lord Clark of Saltwood, 1980 (WA1980.135)

.

11 SLEEPING POSITIONS 1940–1

Second shelter sketchbook, p.45
Pencil, wax crayon, coloured crayon, watercolour, wash, pen and ink on paper · 20.4 × 16.5 cm
Inscribed u.c. *Angular [...] figures covered with coats*
The Henry Moore Foundation: gift of Irina Moore, 1977

12 SLEEPING SHELTERER 1940–1

Second shelter sketchbook, p.69
Pencil, wax crayon, coloured crayon, watercolour, wash, gouache on paper · 20.4 × 16.5 cm
The Henry Moore Foundation: gift of Irina Moore, 1977

13 STUDY FOR 'SHELTER SLEEPERS' 1940–1

Second shelter sketchbook, p.84
Pencil, wax crayon, coloured crayon, pastel, watercolour, wash, pen and ink on paper · 20.4 × 16.5 cm
Inscribed u.r. *mother & child / sleeping /* [child crossed out]
The Henry Moore Foundation: gift of Irina Moore, 1977

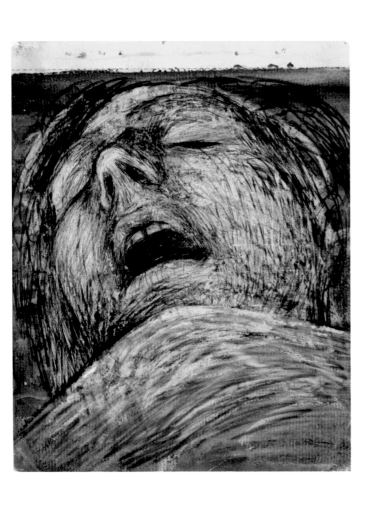

14 FIGURE IN A SHELTER 1941

Pencil, wax crayon, coloured crayon, chalk, watercolour,
wash, pen and ink on paper · 37.9 × 56.1 cm
Inscribed l.r. *Moore* / 41
The Hepworth Wakefield: presented by the Contemporary
Art Society, 1941

15 SHELTER DRAWING: THREE FATES 1941

Pencil, wax crayon, coloured crayon, wash, pen and ink on paper
38.1 × 55.9 cm
Inscribed l.r. *Moore / 41*
Royal Pavilion & Museums, Brighton & Hove

16 GROUP OF SEATED FIGURES 1941

Pencil, wax crayon, coloured crayon, watercolour wash, gouache, pen and ink on paper
35.9 × 43.2 cm
Inscribed l.l. *Moore / 41.*
The Henry Moore Foundation: acquired 2005 in memory of Joanna Drew CBE

17 MINER RESTING 1941

Coalmining notebook A, 1941–2
Pencil and crayon on paper · 12.7 × 20.0 cm
Inscribed l.r. *Miner resting*
The Henry Moore Foundation: gift of the artist, 1977

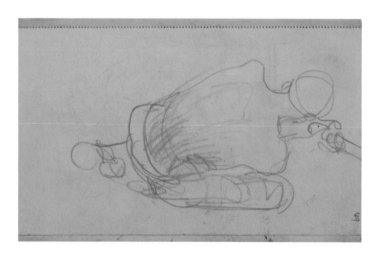

18 MINER WORKING 1941

Coalmining notebook A, 1941–2
Pencil on paper · 12.7 × 20.0 cm
The Henry Moore Foundation: gift of the artist, 1977

19 FOUR STUDIES OF MINERS AT THE COALFACE 1942

Pencil, wax crayon, coloured crayon, watercolour, wash, pen and ink, gouache on paper
36.5 × 56.2 cm · Inscribed l.r. *Moore / 42.*
The Henry Moore Foundation: acquired 1984

Post-War Sculpture

The streamlined naturalistic forms of Moore's monumental *Three Standing Figures*, 1948, in Battersea Park (cat.20 and fig.53) are a development of the draped women in his shelter and other wartime drawings, with their small, stylized heads and almost expressionless faces. David Sylvester commented that 'in Moore's sculpture drapery is there to evoke certain kinds of art rather than life. In sculptures of the 40s, it tends to evoke the Gothic. From the time of Moore's visit to Greece in 1951, it tends to evoke the classical.'[10] The symbolism of groups of three figures in Christian iconography and classical mythology – the women at the foot of the Cross, the Fates, the three Graces and so on – is here given a contemporary edge: the women's eyes look up anxiously, as if they are expecting an air raid.

There are undertones of anxiety and vulnerability as well as aggression in some of the reclining figures (cat.23), and openwork and helmet heads (cats 21, 22 and 25) that Moore made in the early 1950s. Representing man as a wholesome, undamaged being was problematical for a number of European artists – not least, Francis Bacon – who felt humanist values were severely tested by the revelations of the Holocaust and by the escalating threat of nuclear war. Some artists looked outside the Western tradition or to non-human sources. According to David Sylvester, *Openwork Head No. 2*, 1950 (cat.21), was inspired by a small Benin bronze of a tiger mauling a man that Moore owned.[11] Viewed from certain angles, *Animal Head*, 1951 (cat.24), resembles a grotesque human skull. *Reclining Figure: Festival*, 1951 (cat.23), commissioned for the Festival of Britain, is hardly a comforting, maternal sight. A masterpiece of Moore's new skeletal, transparent style, in which space and form are 'sculpturally inseparable',[12] the figure is tense, unrelaxed, wary, its head scooped out into a shape resembling an enormous telephone receiver. As if to emphasize that maternity is not always idyllic, in *Maquette for Mother and Child*, 1952 (cat.26), Moore shows the mother attempting to stop the child from attacking and devouring her breast – a vivid illustration of Freud's theory of infantile sexuality.

Fig.53 | *Three Standing Figures*, 1948
Darley Dale stone
Battersea Park, London.

20 THREE STANDING FIGURES 1945

Plaster with surface colour · H 21.6 cm
The Henry Moore Foundation: gift of the artist, 1977

21 OPENWORK HEAD NO. 2 1950

Bronze edition of 1 · H 40.0 cm
The Hepworth Wakefield: gift of The Contemporary Art Society, 1952

22 MAQUETTE FOR STRAPWORK HEAD 1950

Bronze edition of 9 + 1
Cast: Fiorini, London 1972 · H 10.0 cm
The Henry Moore Foundation: gift of the artist, 1977

Bronze edition of 5 + 1 · L 228.5 cm
Cast: The Art Bronze Foundry, London
Scottish National Gallery of Modern Art, Edinburgh:
presented by the Arts Council of Great Britain
through the Scottish Arts Council, 1969

24 ANIMAL HEAD 1951

Bronze edition of 8 + 1 · L 30.5 cm
The Henry Moore Foundation: gift of the artist, 1977

25 HELMET HEAD AND SHOULDERS 1952

Bronze edition of 10 + 2 · H 20.5 cm
Cast: The Art Bronze Foundry, London
Tate, London: presented by the artist, 1978

26 MAQUETTE FOR MOTHER AND CHILD 1952

Bronze edition of 9 + 1 · H 21.6 cm
Cast: The Art Bronze Foundry, London
The Provost and Fellows of Worcester College, Oxford

Post-War Drawings

These two beautiful drawings show the radically different approaches to the human form that Moore developed concurrently after the war. *Four Figures in a Setting*, 1948 (cat.27), grew out of the naturalistic shelter drawings and found its sculptural expression in the draped standing figures in Battersea Park (cat.20), and the family groups of the late 1940s and early 1950s. *Sculpture in Landscape*, 1951 (cat.28), by contrast, is a striking example of Moore's more synthetic, 'opened-out' idiom, in which solid and void interpenetrate, the bodily forms themselves resemble rock formations, and the head is distorted into a featureless protuberance or gaping mask. What unites the two images is a feeling of alienation: figures isolated in their environments, whether prison-like interior or barren, hostile landscape, waiting for something to happen..

27 FOUR FIGURES IN A SETTING 1948

Pencil, wax crayon, watercolour wash, pen and ink
on paper · 57.0 × 76.5 cm
Inscribed l.r. *Moore / 48*
The Henry Moore Foundation: acquired 2011

28 SCULPTURE IN LANDSCAPE 1951

Pencil, wax crayon, pastel, charcoal, watercolour wash, pen
and ink on paper · 58.4 × 48.9 cm
Inscribed l.r. *Moore, / 51*
The Henry Moore Foundation: acquired 2010

29 KING AND QUEEN 1952–3

Bronze edition of 5 + 2 · H 164.0 cm
Cast: Fiorini, London
The Henry Moore Foundation: acquired 1991

Heroic Works of the 1950s

In the 1950s Moore introduced the male figure into his sculpture for the first time. The broad backs of the king in *King and Queen*, 1952–3 (cat.29), and of *Warrior with Shield*, 1953–4 (fig.54), recall some of his wartime drawings of miners at work underground, stripped to the waist and seen from behind (cat.19). Unlike these studies, however, the artist made no attempt to convey energy or movement in *King and Queen*. Inspired by a hieratic Egyptian sculpture of a seated court official and his wife in the British Museum, the king and queen are remote, inscrutable authority figures in the same way that Bacon's enthroned Popes are (cat.58). Immediately after completing *King and Queen* Moore started work on *Warrior with Shield*, the first single, discrete male figure in his sculpture. Moore described the warrior's head, which was also produced as an independent bronze (cat.30), as having 'a blunted and bull-like power but also a sort of dumb animal acceptance and forbearance of pain'.[13] On a visit to Moore in 1960, Stephen Spender records seeing in the studio 'a study for a head':

I asked him how he arrived at these heads with great clefts down the whole of the centre. He explained that when he was a boy in his Yorkshire mining village he used to go with two or three other boys to the slaughter house and see animals being killed. The men who killed them used to do this by hitting them with a mallet in the centre of the forehead. If they hit in exactly the right spot the animal died at once, but if they didn't succeed in doing this they had to hit two or three times more ... Henry said this was a terrible experience that had haunted him all his life.

When he did his statue of the warrior he wanted to suggest a stricken dehumanised head, and he found himself ... influenced by his memories of the axed animals in the slaughter house.[14]

Bacon likewise was fascinated by the killing of animals. 'I've always been very moved by pictures about slaughterhouses and meat, and to me they belong very much to the whole thing of the Crucifixion', he told David Sylvester in 1962.[15]

The rich and varied surfaces of Moore's mature figurative sculptures point to an engagement with classical antiquity, partly as a result of his trip to Greece in 1951, and with the work of Michelangelo – interests he shared with Francis Bacon. This development was closely related to the fact that Moore was now working largely in plaster for casting into bronze. As he said about *Warrior with Shield*, 'all the knowledge gained from the life drawing and modelling I had done years before came back to me with great pleasure'.[16] *Warrior with Shield* and *Falling*

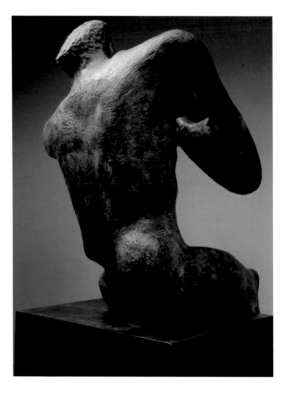

Fig.54 | *Warrior with Shield*, 1953–4 · Bronze

and *Falling Warrior*, 1956–7 (cat.32), demonstrate a new concern with movement, appropriate to the subject of a man in action, and the importance of the viewer walking around the sculpture to appreciate its constantly changing appearance. According to David Sylvester, Moore realized after finishing *Falling Warrior* that its legs were a transposition of Christ's legs in Michelangelo's *Rondanini Pietà*.[17] The much smaller *Fragment Figure*, 1957 (cat.33), has been interpreted as a homage to the pedimental sculptures from the Parthenon in the British Museum.[18]

The power of the fragment is at its most affecting in the truncated *Woman*, 1957–8 (cat.35), which may have originated in Moore's fascination with the 'Venus' of Willendorf and other prehistoric fertility statuettes. Moore explained that the 'smallness of the head [was] necessary to emphasise the massiveness of the body'.[19] *Woman* is placed on a shallow pedestal. In other sculptures of this period, Moore, perhaps following Michelangelo, experimented with seating his figures on a variety of architectural features such as steps, a ledge (cat.34), a bench and even against a wall.

In the *Three Upright Motives* Moore's new haptic language of soft passages alternating with hard, of rough with smooth, of flesh and bone, is seen at its most magisterial. In 1955 he made a total of thirteen maquettes for the *Upright Motive* series, five of which were enlarged to full size. Nos 1, 2 and 7 are usually grouped together, as here (cat.31), with *Upright Motive No.1*, the so-called 'Glenkiln Cross', in the centre. Moore later said that he:

started by balancing different forms one above the other – with results rather like North American totem poles – but as I continued the attempt gained more unity and also perhaps became more organic – and then one in particular ... took on the shape of a crucifix – a kind of worn-down body and a cross merged into one ...

Three of them grouped themselves together, and in my mind, assumed the aspect of a crucifixion scene as though framed against the sky above Golgotha.[20]

Moore incised the cross with a ladder and other instruments of the Passion. Apart from its Christian associations, the 'Glenkiln Cross' is the most phallic of the *Upright Motives*.

30 WARRIOR'S HEAD 1953

Plaster · H 25.5 cm
The Henry Moore Foundation: gift of the artist, 1977

31 THREE UPRIGHT MOTIVES:

NO.1: GLENKILN CROSS 1955

Bronze edition of 6 + 1 · H 332.7 cm
Cast: Hermann Noack, Berlin
Tate, London: gift of the artist, 1978

NO.2 1955–6

Bronze edition of 5 + 1 · H 335.3 cm
Cast: H.H. Martyn, Cheltenham
Tate, London: gift of the artist, 1978

NO.7 1955–6

Bronze edition of 5 + 1 · H 340.4 cm
Cast: H.H. Martyn, Cheltenham
Tate, London: gift of the artist, 1978

32 FALLING WARRIOR 1956–7

Bronze edition of 10 + 1 · L 154 cm
Cast: Fiorini, London
Tate, London: gift of the artist, 1978

33 FRAGMENT FIGURE 1957

Bronze edition of 10 · L 19.0 cm
Cast: The Art Bronze Foundry, London
Ashmolean Museum, University of Oxford: bequeathed by Lady Hendy, 1993
(WA1993.330)

34 SEATED FIGURE ON LEDGE 1957

Bronze edition of 4 + 1 · H 26.0 cm
The Henry Moore Foundation: gift of the artist, 1977

35 WOMAN 1957–8

Bronze edition of 8 + 1 · H 144.1 cm
Cast: Hermann Noack, Berlin
Tate, London: presented by the artist, 1978

State of Flux

In the 1950s Moore produced a series of mixed media drawings of heads in which facial features are almost obliterated by a network of thick black brushstrokes culminating in jagged edges suggesting a crown of thorns (cats 36 and 37). Kenneth Clark thought these heads were 'the ultimate antitypes of the placid, ideal heads' and were 'drawn with a ferocity that proves how much Moore's inner demon sees the human head as a terrible and fascinating enemy'.[21] Moore's earlier, more naturalistic, drawing *Tragic Head* (fig.55) depicts the anquished expression of a woman who has experienced prolonged suffering. Given its date, 1946, it may have been based on a news photograph of a 'Displaced Person' or Holocaust survivor. The armoured *Head* of 1959 (cat.38) may have been the 'study for a head' with a cleft down its centre which Stephen Spender saw in Moore's studio in 1960. In *Square Reclining Forms*, 1961–2 (cat.39), Moore appears to come close to the disintegration of the body into a state of flux that we find in some of Francis Bacon's paintings.

Fig.55 | *Tragic Head* 1946, Private Collection

36 HEAD 1950/1958

Pencil, wax crayon, coloured crayon, pastel, watercolour wash, brush and ink
29.0 × 24.0 cm · Inscribed l.l. *Moore / 58*
The Henry Moore Foundation: gift of the artist, 1977

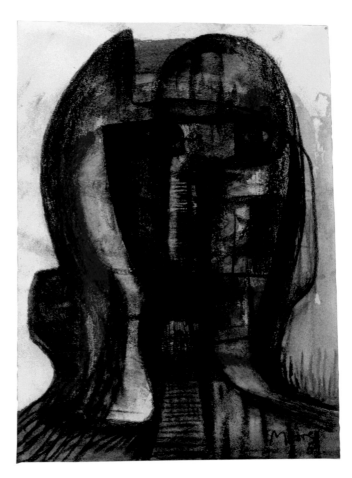

37 HEAD 1950/1958

Pencil, wax crayon, coloured crayon, watercolour wash, brush and ink
24.0 × 29.0 cm · Inscribed l.r. *Moore / 58*
The Henry Moore Foundation: gift of the artist, 1977

38 HEAD 1959

Pastel, wash · 26.0 × 19.7 cm
Inscribed l.r. *Moore / 59.*
The Henry Moore Foundation: gift of the artist, 1977

39 SQUARE RECLINING FORMS 1961–2

Sketchbook 1961–2, p.16
Pencil, wax crayon, coloured crayon, watercolour wash,
ballpoint pen, felt-tipped pen, pen and ink on paper
29.2 × 24.0 cm
Inscribed (later) l.r. *Moore / 61.* and u.c.*Square reclining figures*
The Henry Moore Foundation: gift of the artist, 1977

A Late Sculpture

Continuing the analogy with Bacon, the sinuous form of *Three-Quarter Figure: Lines*, 1980 (cat.40), emphasized by the sectional lines that criss-cross its surface, bears a resemblance to the right-hand panel of Bacon's *Three Studies for a Crucifixion*, 1962 (Solomon R. Guggenheim Museum, New York). Bacon based this image on Cimabue's *Crucifixion*, 1272–4, in Florence which he had inverted in his mind and which he famously compared to 'a worm crawling down the cross'.[22]

40 THREE QUARTER FIGURE: LINES 1980

Plaster · H 84.0 cm
The Henry Moore Foundation: acquired 1993

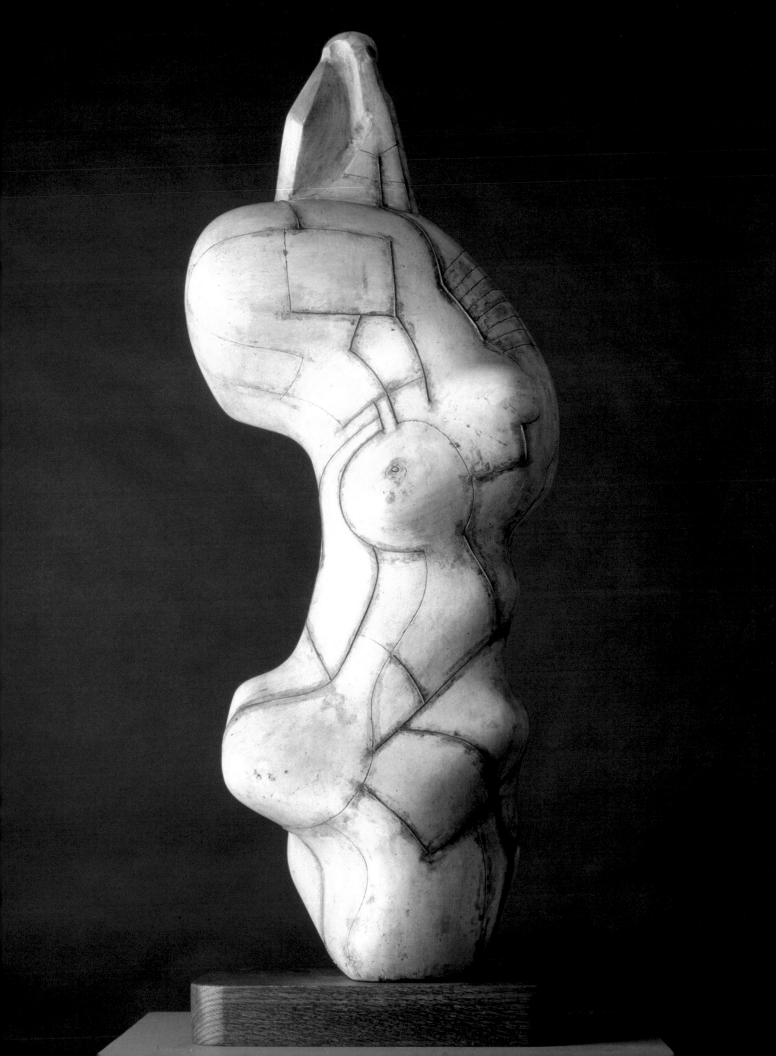

41 CRUCIFIXION I 1982

Charcoal, wax crayon, watercolour, chinagraph, pencil,
ballpoint pen on paper · 25.3 × 17.9 cm
Inscribed l.l. *Moore*
The Henry Moore Foundation: acquired 1987

Last Drawings

Moore, like Bacon, was a non-believer. He once said
that 'artists do not need religion for art is religion
itself'.[23] The only commission he accepted from the
Church was the *Madonna and Child*, 1943–4, for
St Matthew's, Northampton, about which he had
serious misgivings. He had similar doubts when
later asked to do a Crucifixion, but conceded that
'the Crucifixion is such a universal theme that I
may attempt it one day'.[24] This is similar to Bacon's
remark that 'the Crucifixion [is] a magnificent armature on which you can hang all types of feeling and
sensation'.[25]

   A few years before his death, in his eighty-fifth
year and in failing health, Moore made three
drawings of the Crucifixion (cats 41–3). All three
are loosely based on Michelangelo's late Crucifixion
drawings which he revered. Cats 41 and 42 both show
the Y-shaped Cross that Michelangelo introduced
(for example, in drawings in the British Museum and
the Royal Collection, Windsor), so that Christ's arms
would be raised high above His shoulders, intensi-
fying the sense of strain and suffering.[26] The position
of the body in cat.43 is close to the British Museum
drawing of *Christ on the Cross between the Virgin and
St John*, c.1555–64, although, instead of being nailed
to the Cross by His hands, Moore depicts Christ's left
arm looping back over the crossbeam, as if hanging
from it or trying to stop Himself from sliding down it.

42 CRUCIFIXION II 1982

Pencil, charcoal, wax crayon, watercolour wash, pastel wash,
chinagraph, ballpoint pen on paper · 25.3 × 17.4 cm
Inscribed l.r. *Moore*
The Henry Moore Foundation: acquired 1987

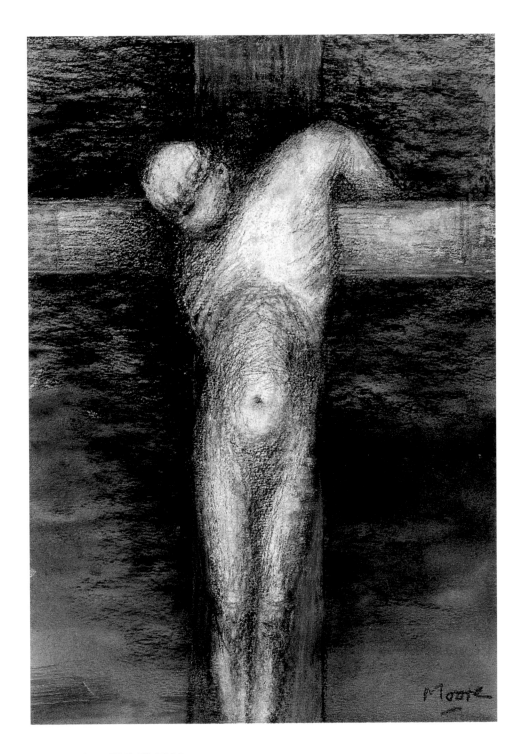

43 CRUCIFIXION III 1982

Wax crayon, charcoal, pencil, watercolour wash,
ink wash on paper · 35.5 × 25.3 cm
Inscribed l.r. *Moore*
Mr. Richard Clark Colton, Jr.

BACON
MOORE

44 COMPOSITION 1933

Gouache on paper · 52.2 × 39.7 cm
The Henry Moore Family Collection

Since a mere fourteen paintings and drawings
from the first fifteen years of Bacon's career were
thought to have survived his ruthless destruction
of his earliest work, the re-emergence of this
hitherto undocumented gouache in 2009 was an
exciting occurrence.

   While *Composition* has several features in
common with Bacon's contemporaneous works on
paper, such as the tongue-and-groove floorboards
and walls (these are also found in the paintings of his
mentor, Roy de Maistre), the vivid, painterly inter-
jections of red, yellow and white, which disrupt the
relatively well-behaved geometry, were a significant
departure: they portend, in some respects, the free,
vigorous brushstrokes associated with Bacon's oil
paintings from 1949 onwards. Like Moore, he was
striving to escape from the influence of Picasso, in a
work of unusual vitality for 1933 that gives a tanta-
lising glimpse of a direction Bacon did not pursue
until sixteen years later.

45 STUDIO INTERIOR 1936

Pastel on paper · 24.0 × 35.0 cm
Private Collection, courtesy of Hauser & Wirth

Studio Interior was dated around 1934 by Ronald Alley, who noted that the placing of the object on a pedestal (left) anticipated a significant aspect of *Three Studies for Figures at the Base of a Crucifixion*, 1944. The adjustment in date here has been made because the drawing is clearly a reworking of the basic pictorial elements in Picasso's studies for *Jeune femme dessinant dans un intérieur*, 1935; these were reproduced in a special edition of *Cahiers d'Art, Picasso 1930–1935*, published early in 1936.

Studio Interior also embodies the first, or certainly the most overt, announcement of Bacon's inclusion of sculpture in his iconography. The central biomorph, like its antecedents in Picasso's oeuvre, is a distinctly sculptural form, while the placement of the object on the left (presumably itself a sculpture) on a pedestal is balanced by the canvas on an easel (right), a prescient Bacon *paragone*. Some of Picasso's 'cabana' paintings, made in Cannes and Dinard between 1927 and 1932, were themselves conceived as studies for massive sculptures.

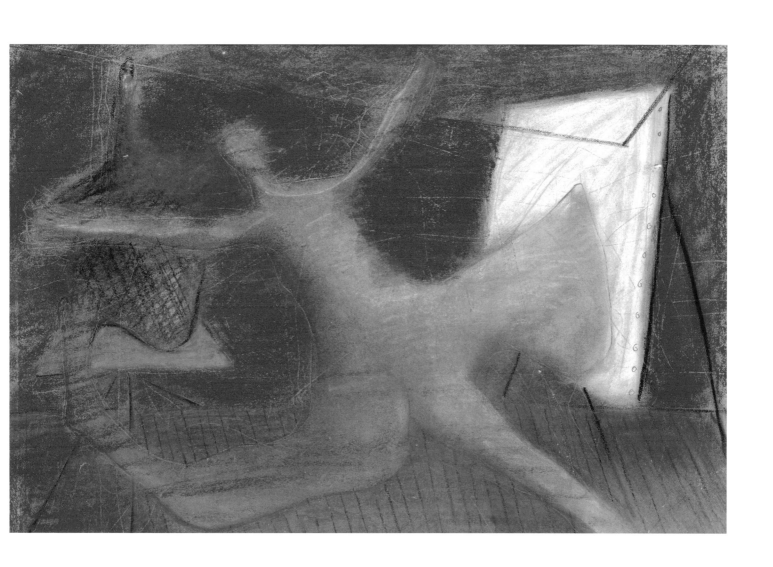

46 HEAD II 1949

Oil on canvas · 80.5 × 60.0 cm
Ulster Museum, National Museums of Northern Ireland,
Belfast

Head II was the second in a series of six heads that
Bacon painted in 1948 and 1949. Its stretcher was
made in Cannes, and it may well, like *Head I*, have
been begun, or even completed, while Bacon was
living in Monaco. It invites comparison with Henry
Moore's similarly disquieting wartime helmet heads,
in that the distortions and dehumanizing of both can
be seen as a reflection of contemporary anxieties.
In its physical substance the painting is the most
extreme manifestation of Bacon's stated desire 'to
paint like Velazquez but with the texture of a hippo-
potamus skin',[1] an aim that in *Head* II is conveyed in
the painterly marks in the lower register against the
dense, leathery impasto of the grey ground.

What Bacon intended with this image is, as so
often in his paintings, not easy to determine. It may
have been inspired by the decapitated head of St John
Baptist, for which there was ample art-historical
precedent, or perhaps by T.S. Eliot's line in 'The Love
Song of J. Alfred Prufrock': 'Though I have seen my
head (grown slightly bald) brought in upon a platter'.
In 1949, when *Head* II was purchased by Robin
Ironside on behalf of the Contemporary Arts Society,
it was known as 'Laughing Man', yet the anguished
expression of the mouth is more a sardonic grimace,
an existential half-animal howl that anticipated Allen
Ginsberg's angry, eponymous poem.

47 PAINTING 1950

Oil on canvas · 198.0 × 152.0 cm
Leeds Art Fund (Leeds Art Gallery)

Formally, *Painting*, 1950, is unique in Bacon's output. A figure and its 'shadow' (stooping, ambiguously, and behind the circular metal rail) move silently sidewards, in parallel to our gaze, passing in front of what appears to be a vividly striped curtain hung on a brass rail, perhaps in a bath-house. While in some respects *Painting*, 1950, can be related to Bacon's switch to the human body as his main subject in 1949, in others it stands as one of his distinctly *sui generis* paintings. Its most conspicuous deviation from Bacon's contemporary manner was in its vivid palette and planar spatial organization. As David Sylvester pointed out, it also marked a return to the heroic dimensions of Bacon's *Painting*, 1946; these two remained for many years the largest canvases Bacon had completed.

Ronald Alley noted a loose correspondence with Eadweard Muybridge's photo sequences of men walking (it was probably a case of Bacon conflating aspects of several images), but only in recent years have scholars attempted to further penetrate some of the mysteries that this painting resolutely resists disclosing; future investigation of the significance of the many pentimenti may eventually reveal vital clues.

The shimmering bands of red and blue at the top and bottom are comparable with the rectangles of pulsing colour that Mark Rothko developed in 1949; while this putative analogy may be entirely coincidental, Rothko was, tantalisingly, in London in August 1950, shortly before Bacon began *Painting*, 1950. Rebecca Daniels has demonstrated that Bacon borrowed details from Walter Sickert's drawing *Conversation*, c.1909 (Royal College of Art, London), which he would certainly have encountered at the college in 1950. To this list I would add Matthew Smith's *Nude in a Chair*, c.1915 (Corporation of London), and *Fitzroy Street Nude No. 1*, 1916 (Tate Gallery, London); Bacon and Smith were close at this time, and these paintings could have informed both Bacon's palette and, with Michelangelo's *Dying Slave* and the wax model in the Victoria and Albert Museum, the 'Ariadne' pose of the arched arm.

The untypically formal presentation of the painting was partly derived from Matisse, who was another possible source for both the odalisque pose and the brightly striped curtain; but irrespective of the manifold pictorial absorptions, *Painting*, 1950, is characterized predominantly by the Michelangelesque monumentality of the principal figure and Bacon's correspondingly voluptuous painting of his anatomy.

48 MAN KNEELING IN GRASS 1952

Oil on canvas · 198.0 × 137.0 cm
Private Collection

At the end of May 1952 Bacon returned from the second trip he had made to South Africa, on which he had been accompanied by his new lover, Peter Lacy. The nude man in *Study of Figure in Landscape*, 1952, is based on a photograph that Bacon took of Lacy in South Africa, and *Man Kneeling in Grass* (the figure is stooping or crawling, more than kneeling) is also likely to have been inspired by Lacy, even though the figure, in common with most of Bacon's nude males at this time, is of a more bulky build than Lacy's. The pose of the shadowy figure still visible above the crawling man's arched back in the present painting is similar to that of Lacy in *Study of Figure in Landscape*.

Bacon had been transfixed by the sight of eland and baboons moving about the bushy scrubland of Northern Transvaal, and the grasslands of the veldt were transposed into many of his paintings in 1952. In *Man Kneeling in Grass* we see one of his earliest conflations of man and animal; the pose of the figure probably relied partly on Eadweard Muybridge's sequence of a striding baboon, and is also related to Marius Maxwell's photograph of a collapsing rhinoceros in *Stalking Big Game with a Camera* (1925), a book that was one of Bacon's most fertile sources of imagery.

The rapid, arcing strokes that delineate the grass are typical of Bacon's African and Côte d'Azur paintings of this period; grass was a potent symbol for Bacon, who said of Van Gogh 'when he painted a field he was able to give you the violence of grass'.

49 STUDY FOR PORTRAIT III
(AFTER THE LIFE-MASK OF WILLIAM BLAKE) 1955

Oil on canvas · 61.0 × 51.0 cm
Private Collection

In order to be near to Peter Lacy, who lived at Hurst,
Berkshire, Bacon spent much of his time in 1954
and 1955 in hotels and houses in Henley-on-Thames.
Among the friends he made there was the composer
Gerard Schurmann, who was married to Vivien
Hind; her father, A.M. Hind, had been Keeper of the
Department of Prints at the British Museum. Another
mutual friend in Henley, significantly, was the
William Blake scholar and collector, George Goyder.

In 1954 Schurmann asked Bacon to provide a cover
illustration for the score of his *Nine Poems of William
Blake*, although in the event none of the music was
published until much later. Bacon gave the first
three in the series (including *Study for Portrait* III) to
Schurmann, but borrowed them back to include in his
exhibition at the Hanover Gallery, London, in June
1955, whereupon all three were sold at the private
view. Bacon eventually painted seven variations on
this theme, five of which survive, and their painterly
inventiveness, within the constraints of the subject
matter, is extremely impressive: he had turned what
might have been an almost academic exercise into
hauntingly evocative images of human isolation.

Bacon painted Schurmann's portrait in 1969, and
it was reproduced on the cover of the sheet music
for Schurmann's orchestral homage to the artist, *Six
Studies of Francis Bacon*, published in 1969.

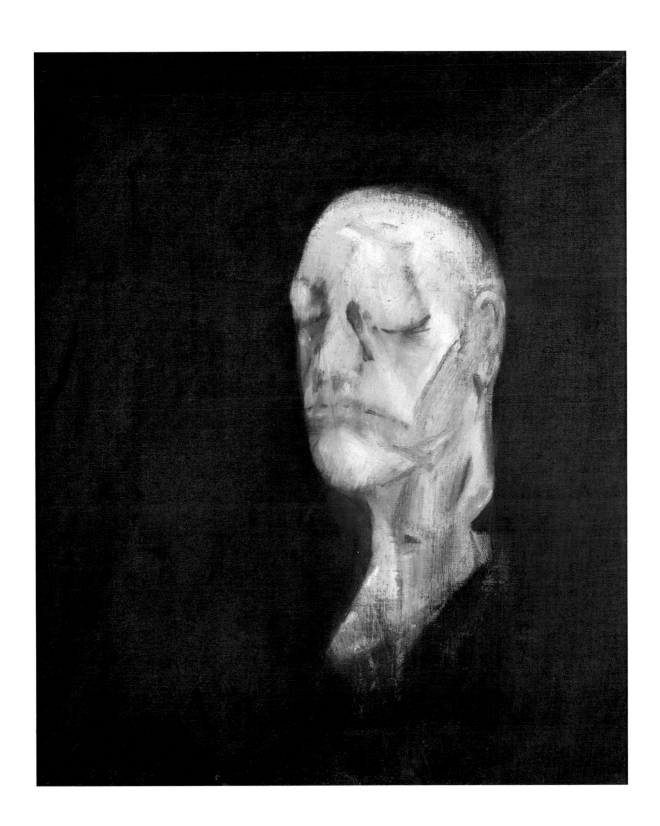

50 LYING FIGURE 1959

Oil on canvas · 198.5 × 142.6 cm
New Walk Art Gallery and Museum, Leicester

Lying Figure, 1959, announced Bacon's expanding repertory of exaggerated limb positions. Five paintings survive from the sub-genre initiated with this work, in which a somewhat ungracefully inverted nude lies on a couch with one leg raised and the other bent at the knee, with the right arm outstretched.

In October 1958 Bacon switched dealers, from the Hanover Gallery to the prestigious Marlborough Fine Art Ltd, London; almost a year later, with his first solo exhibition looming and few paintings completed, he moved to St Ives in order to paint without London's distractions. Shortly before moving to St Ives he seems to have resolved to reinvent his paintings, to relaunch himself with radically new material, while still 'mocking grandeur' as Robert Melville put it in the catalogue of Bacon's first Marlborough exhibition, in March/April 1960. *Lying Figure* was included in this exhibition (it was then titled *Lying Figure No. I*), together with *Two Figures in a Room* (cat.51).

51 TWO FIGURES IN A ROOM 1959

Oil on canvas · 198.0 × 140.5 cm
Robert and Lisa Sainsbury Collection,
Sainsbury Centre for Visual Arts, University of East Anglia

Two Figures in a Room can be situated as a final
working out of the theme of a crouching nude,
together with its 'shadow', or a secondary figure,
that had obsessed Bacon since he painted *Study for
Crouching Nude*, 1952 (Detroit Institute of Arts); as
Bacon remarked, 'Images breed one from another'.
Subsequently he explored different expressions of his
preoccupation with 'death shadowing life'.

All the crouching nudes of approximately this
configuration stemmed from fusions of a photograph
of the crouching woman in Matisse's *Bather with a
Turtle*, 1908 (MoMA, New York), and a photograph
of a cameraman mauled by a lion in Africa, taken by
Gonzague Dreux in 1947; the photograph, originally
published in *Nuit et Jour*, was re-run in *Picture Post*
on 9 August 1947. The second, cropped figure in
Two Figures in a Room does not appear elsewhere
in Bacon's paintings, at least in such a concrete and
eroticized form.

The palette of *Two Figures in a Room* and the green
outline of the figures is reminiscent of the double
register in 3-D colour printing; Bacon owned one of
the first 3-D books produced in Britain, J.E. Burns'
Adventures in Wildest Africa (1949).

52 HEAD OF A MAN 1959

Oil on canvas · 48.0 × 46.5 cm
Private Collection

Although Bacon had painted heads throughout his
career (see, for example, *Head II*, cat.46) it was not
until 1958 that he became a committed painter of
head-and-shoulders portraits, at approximately life
size. Initially these were painted in a 61.0 × 51.0 cm
format, but *Head of a Man*, 1959, is slightly larger than
the dimensions which Bacon adopted for the small
portraits (35.5 × 30.5 cm) that accounted for a significant proportion of his output between 1961 and 1990.

In evolving these more individuated portraits,
Bacon may again have been looking at Rodin. Both
the energy of Bacon's brushstrokes and expressive
handling of the materials in *Head of a Man*, 1959,
are comparable with Rodin's technique in the
early *Man with Broken Nose* and the later *Iris; Large
Head*, a cast of which was in the Victoria and Albert
Museum collection.

Head of a Man was painted during Bacon's sojourn
in St Ives; it depicts Ron Belton, who had gone to
St Ives with Bacon in September 1959. According to
Lucian Freud, it was painted from life; Bacon also
painted Cecil Beaton from life in 1960, but destroyed
the canvas when Beaton reacted badly to it, and
subsequently he seldom, if ever, painted again from a
live model.

53 SKETCH OF A RECLINING FIGURE c.1959

Ballpoint pen and oil on paper · 23.5 × 15.4 cm
Tate, London. Purchased with assistance from the National Lottery
through the Heritage Lottery Fund, the Art Fund and a group of
anonymous donors in memory of Mario Tazzoli, 1998

A majority of the approximately seventy sketches by
Bacon that are known to survive date from around
1959. Nearly all of them are associated with the
fundamental reconfigurations of gesture he was
implementing at that time, and although some are
related to photographs of boxers or to Muybridge's
motion studies, Rodin is a significant presence
in many.

 Bacon denied making drawings, and whether
their emergence (almost entirely after Bacon's death)
implies that he had utilized preliminary sketches
more consistently throughout his career remains a
matter of debate. This is one of the most elaborate of
the drawings that are currently known, and the most
prescriptive of a linked painting, *Untitled (Reclining
Figure)*, c.1959 (Private Collection).

54 SKETCH OF A TURNING FIGURE c.1962

Ink and oil on paper · 25.1 × 18.8 cm
Private Collection

This sketch, as the signature on the very similar reverse of the sheet indicates, was given by Bacon to Lucian Freud in 1972.

Several related sketches in black paint exist, most significantly a group on the endpapers of a catalogue of an exhibition of the Belarusian-born expressionist painter Chaïm Soutine held at MOMA, New York, in 1950; like this sketch of a turning figure, their calligraphic style reflects Bacon's interest in cave art and in the drawings of the Belgian-born French artist Henri Michaux. The impressive illustrations by Bacon's friend Louis le Brocquy for *The Táin* (1969) are in a comparable style. Bacon had painted similarly schematic figures in the backgrounds of several paintings he made between 1950 and 1952, such as *Fragment of a Crucifixion*, 1950.

Soutine's portraits were influential on the rubbery, pliable anatomies of figures that Bacon painted in 1961 and 1962, and there are compelling reasons for ascribing these sketches to the same period, in view of their further similarities with the coeval paintings of turning figures.

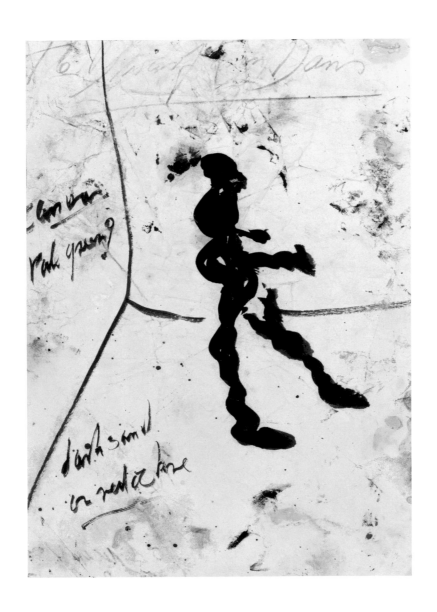

55 SEATED FIGURE 1962

Oil on canvas · 198.0 × 142.0 cm
Private Collection

This painting shows Bacon's lover Peter Lacy, naked and sitting cross-legged in a red room. The profile head was based partly on a series of John Deakin's photographs of Lacy, taken in London around 1960. The unstable, fluid pose of the figure recalls Michelangelo's figures (especially *Evening*) in the Medici Chapel, Florence, which appear almost about to slide from the cornices of the curved pediments on which they rest. In its extra animation, Bacon's figure extended his recent adaptations of Rodin's sculptures, whose dynamized poses may have influenced the quirkily outstretched leg. Lacy's anvil-like seat resembles the papal thrones from other paintings of the time, such as *Study from Innocent* X, 1962, as well as the structure supporting the flayed carcass in the right-hand panel of *Three Studies for a Crucifixion*, 1962.

Peter Lacy died in May 1962 in Tangier; Bacon learnt of his death on the eve of the opening of his retrospective exhibition at Tate Gallery, London. *Seated Figure* was painted in about March 1962, and was first exhibited that year in *Aspects of Twentieth-Century Art* at Marlborough Fine Art, London, with the title *Study for Portrait (with Mauve Blinds)*. The blinds, with their flimsy pull-cords, were a recurrent device in Bacon's paintings, from *Painting*, 1946, to *Lying Figure in a Mirror*, 1971 (cat.59) and later. The curved space in which Lacy is situated features in several of Bacon's portraits; he later suggested that it may have been a reminiscence of the curved walls of the bay windows in the Georgian house 'Farmleigh', County Laois, one of his childhood homes. The curved wall in *Seated Figure* anticipates that in the left and centre panels of the almost contemporaneous *Three Studies for a Crucifixion*, 1962, and *Seated Figure* was possibly destined originally to be the right panel of this pivotal triptych; in a *mise en abyme* in the background of *Study for a Portrait*, 1967, he alluded, enigmatically, to both versions in a triptych that he sketchily painted on the wall.

Bacon habitually sought to extend themes he had been exploring in his own paintings, and to this end he pinned reproductions of them to the walls of the kitchen area in 7 Reece Mews. Eleven years after *Seated Figure* was completed, he continued to keep reproductions of it on his kitchen wall, which suggests it contained the germ of an idea he intended to develop.

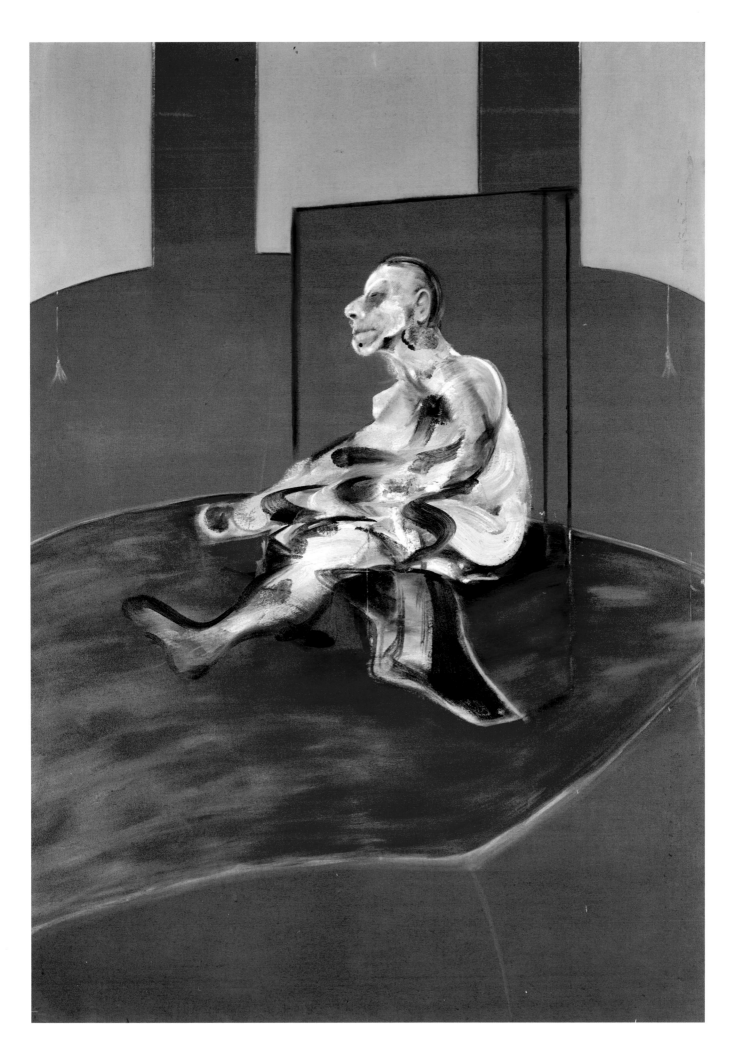

56 PORTRAIT OF HENRIETTA MORAES 1963

Oil on canvas · 165.0 × 142.0 cm
Private Collection

At the beginning of 1963 Bacon painted the first
of a series of nudes of his friend Henrietta Moraes,
entitled *Lying Figure with Hypodermic Syringe*. It
shows Moraes lying upside down on a ticking-covered
mattress, the syringe prominently and rather melo-
dramatically inserted into her right arm. In her auto-
biography Moraes observed that although she did not
use drugs at that time, Bacon's harrowing painting
was curiously prescient of the heroin addiction that
she picked up later.

Both this and *Portrait of Henrietta Moraes*, 1963,
were based on a set of photographs that Bacon had
commissioned from John Deakin, presumably in
1962, of Moraes in a variety of lying and sitting
postures; he adapted these poses for a further eight
paintings of the nude Moraes up to 1969. *Portrait of
Henrietta Moraes*, the first painting of Moraes sitting
on a bed, is arguably the most powerful of them
all; uncompromising and unflinching, stripped of
meretriciousness, it is painted in a vivid palette in
which the intense blood red that borders Moraes'
body is adroitly counterpointed with the off-white
bedsheets. Bacon is often at his best in what are
formally his simplest paintings, and this strangely
beautiful picture is a triumph of directly expressive
and intense brushwork.

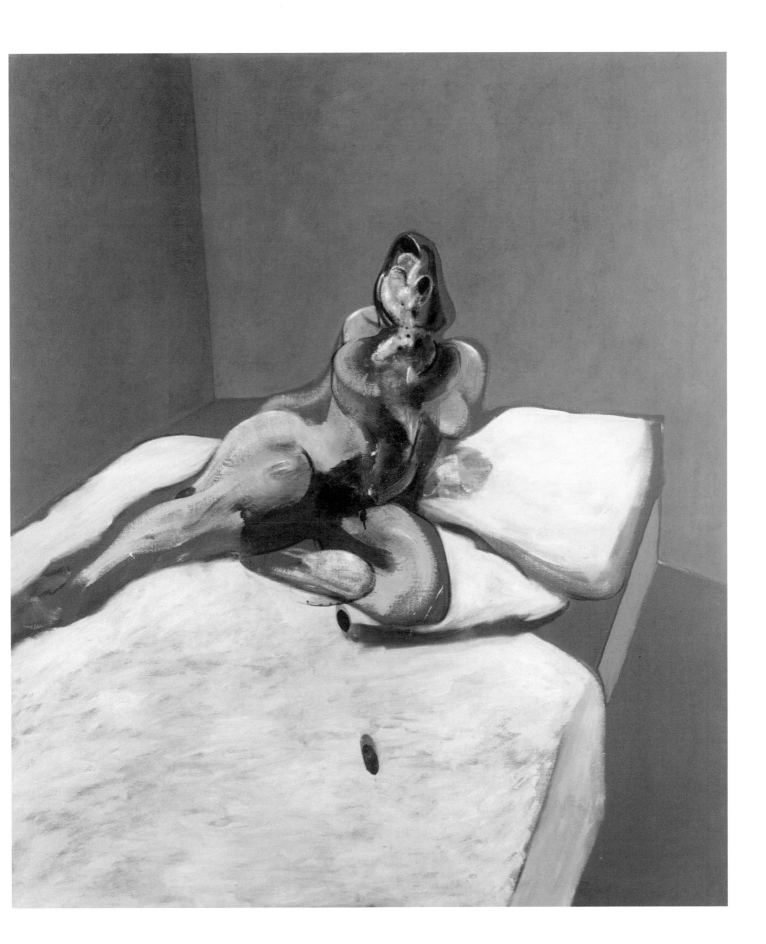

57 PORTRAIT OF MAN WITH GLASSES III 1963

Oil on canvas · 33.5 × 29.0 cm
Private Collection

In his first recorded interview with the art critic David Sylvester, in 1962, Bacon said: 'I think there's a whole area there suggested by Picasso, which in a way has been unexplored, of organic form that relates to the human image but is a complete distortion of it.'[2] No doubt he was referring mainly to the biomorphic forms that had first influenced him in the 1930s and 1940s; but in 1962 he embarked on portraits that could not have evolved outside the legacy of Picasso's 'primitivism' of 1906–7 and the multiple viewpoints of analytical cubism.

Inexplicably, the four versions of *Portrait of Man with Glasses*, the first of Bacon's paintings to reflect his revived interest in Picasso, have tended to be overlooked by critics; perhaps their distorted physiognomies have militated against their easy acceptance. Yet they are among the most effective, if unsettling, of his head-and-shoulders portraits, their impact greatly outweighing their small scale. In nos I and II of the series the head is frontal, whereas in III and IV, which were painted as though from a higher viewpoint, it is turned half to the left.

Bacon invariably made portraits of specific individuals, usually his friends, but the literature is frustratingly silent regarding the identity of the bespectacled man. Sylvester pointed to parallels with Picasso's *Portrait of Jaime Sabartés as a Spanish Grandee*, 1939,[3] and there are affinities throughout the series with the elderly Mahatma Gandhi as he appeared about 1930. Bacon's friend and ophthalmologist Patrick Trevor-Roper is an alternative candidate; it was Trevor-Roper who revealed in his *World Through Blunted Sight* (1970) – a study of artists and defective vision – that he had treated Bacon for astigmatism since the 1940s.

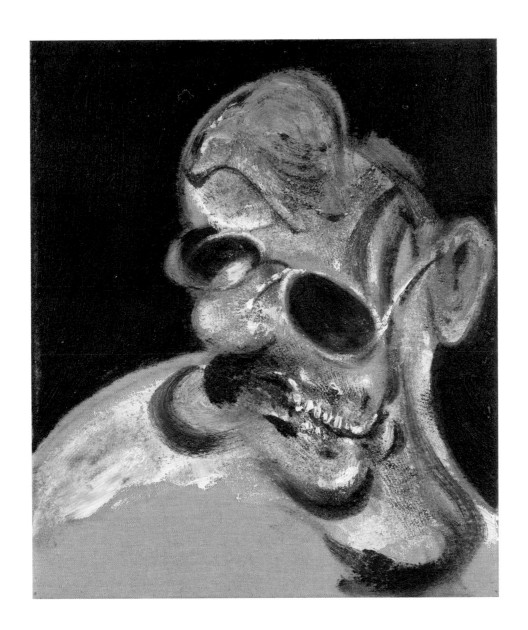

58 STUDY FROM PORTRAIT OF POPE INNOCENT X 1965

Oil on canvas · 198.0 × 147.5 cm
Private Collection

Bacon was understandably anxious to include his *Study from Innocent* X, 1962, in his retrospective exhibition at the Grand Palais, Paris, in 1971. When the loan fell through at the last moment he painted a second version of the painting to replace it; were it not for this exceptional circumstance, the final 'Pope' he painted would have been *Study for a Portrait of Pope Innocent* X, 1965.

By 1966 Bacon had begun his public disavowals of his variations on Velázquez's great portrait, saying 'I've tried, very, very unsuccessfully, to do certain records of it – distorted records. I regret them, because I think they're very silly.'[4] It is plausible that he considered that with *Study from Portrait of Pope Innocent* X, 1965, he had pushed the idea to its limit, in which case it should be considered its ultimate development, his valedictory *coup de grâce*. From the beginning (the earliest extant variation of the Velázquez portrait is *Head* VI, 1949) Bacon had used the Velázquez model not mimetically but as a prelude, as a basis for modification. Besides the 'scream' that he superimposed onto Velázquez's steely, implacable personification of Innocent, he changed the Pope's cassock from red to purple, although this was a fortuitous consequence of Bacon, who was unacquainted with the original, working from black-and-white reproductions; purple was adopted as his aesthetic preference, and not until 1961 did he change to the red blouse. Bacon, who was rigidly if not violently anti-hirsute, had also consistently shorn Innocent of his beard and moustache; if, in these paintings, he was expressing his ambivalence

towards paternal/authority figures, he at least ensured that they were clean-shaven.

As his Pope paintings accreted, Bacon referred increasingly to his own revisions, rather than to the original; sixteen years after his first variation, when this culminated in *Study from Portrait of Pope Innocent* X, he had left Velázquez's meta-text far behind. The most immediately perceptible deviations are the deep space in which this Pope is situated and the abandonment, the erasure, of the vaunted 'scream'. Latterly, Bacon's Popes had been rendered in some of his most brusque treatments, but *Study from Portrait of Pope Innocent X* was their sumptuous antithesis, utilizing the full range of Bacon's techniques, from rich impasto to extemporized brushstrokes of elegant brevity. Irrespective of the Pope's greater distance, the figure has a commanding monumentality that is comparable with Henry Moore's seated figures.

59 LYING FIGURE IN A MIRROR 1971

Oil on canvas · 198.5 × 147.5 cm
Museo de Bellas Artes de Bilbao

The retrospective of 108 of his paintings at the Grand Palais, Paris, in 1971, meant more to the ardently Francophile Bacon than any other exhibition in his life. *Lying Figure in a Mirror* is in many respects a unique work (not least in terms of the unprecedentedly dominant mirror), and was painted specially for the exhibition. Mirrors held a particular fascination for Bacon and they featured prominently in his paintings, but this was the only occasion on which the whole 'image' was painted as a reflection.

Of all the Bacon paintings in the present exhibition, *Lying Figure in a Mirror* most readily invites comparison with Henry Moore's reclining figures. Yet despite the superficial resemblances, such as the space within the figure's raised arm, Moore's investigation of the relationship between mass and the void played no part in Bacon's programme. On the other hand, Moore's 1931 design for a lead sculpture of a not dissimilar lying figure had been reproduced in Herbert Read's *Art Now* (1933), along with the first of Bacon's paintings to be published, *Crucifixion*, 1933; while Bacon was prone to utter dismissive comments about Moore, he was inevitably acquainted with a wide range of his sculpture, not least those from the exhibitions in which they both took part. *Lying Figure in a Mirror* raises another possible analogy with Moore, in that both artists deployed *glissando* surfaces – Bacon with his fluid, smeared paint and Moore with smooth bronze.

Lying Figure in a Mirror is a deceptively sparse painting, with no directly relevant precursors in Bacon's iconography, although there is an affinity with the (cropped) figure on the right in *Two Figures in a Room*, 1959 (cat.51). But despite its immaculate execution and the spare geometry of the spatial matrix, it embodies multiple layers of ulterior meaning. At first sight the unorthodox configuration of the anatomy insists on being interpreted as an eroticized abstraction from the human form, but among Bacon's specific departure points was Michelangelo's *Leda and the Swan*, of which there were copies by Rubens and Rosso Fiorentino in the National Gallery, and a drawing by Rosso in the Royal Academy collection.[5] Bacon deconstructed and re-gendered the rape scene (which is not explicit in *Lying Figure in a Mirror*), reassembling it into a quasi-Vanitas image, transmuting Leda into a kind of Ganymede and the 'armpit' into an anus.

60 TWO STUDIES FROM THE HUMAN BODY 1975

Oil on canvas · 198.0 × 142.0 cm
Private Collection

Bacon frequently made revisions to paintings that he had considered completed. His motivations were manifold and complicated, but most frequently reflected his dissatisfaction with a small passage or detail, or the colour of the background. The changes he made to what became *Two Studies of the Human Body* were more fundamental.

As a close friend of Bacon's, Peter Beard was one of the very few photographers to whom Bacon granted access to his studio, even allowing himself to be photographed together with his paintings. In its first state *Two Studies of the Human Body* was entitled *Figure in Movement* and later *Walking Figure*; but it was known informally as 'The Last Man on Earth', and as such it was recorded in several of Beard's photographs of Bacon moving around the studio. It would appear to have been conceptually entirely resolved, but evidently it evoked for observers events such as the Apollo space mission's moon landing, or a scene from Stanley Kubrick's film *2001: A Space Odyssey* (1968); it may, therefore, have come to embody what for Bacon were disconcertingly narrative connotations, resembling an over-literal portrayal of Nietzschean solipsism. Its chief inspiration, though, was surely T.S. Eliot's lines from 'The Love Song of J. Alfred Prufrock':

> **To have squeezed the universe into a ball**
> **To roll it toward some overwhelming question**
> **To say: 'I am Lazarus, come from the dead ...'**

The isolated figure is loosely based on Eadweard Muybridge's serial photographs of a man throwing a discus, although Bacon may also have been thinking of a classical discobolus as well as the loosely hanging left arm in Rodin's bronze, *La Grande Ombre*. The man's pose resembles that of the figure in the centre panel of *Triptych March 1974*, and *Two Studies of the Human Body* itself is an instance of a panel that had been intended originally as part of a triptych. Bacon's principal alterations were to paint out the ball in the foreground and replace it with a patch of white with randomly applied Letraset, like a fragment of discarded newspaper; and, more fundamentally, the addition of the hunched, simian figure, at the upper right, perched like a sculpture at the junction of two upturned pedestals or socles. Paradoxically, this juxtaposition might be thought to institute an alternative narrative, albeit a particularly oblique one.

61 TWO FIGURES 1975

Oil on canvas · 190.0 × 70.0 cm
Pallant House Gallery. On loan from a private collection, 2010

In 1975 Bacon made a large painting in which one of his 'attendant' figures, a dwarf on a circular stool, sits at the right returning the viewer's gaze, oblivious to, or uninterested in, two upturned figures writhing in a glass cage to the left. In what was probably another example of Bacon's concern about the potential narrative implications set up by the two main images, he proceeded to discard most of the background and cut out just the two principal subjects as separate canvases, each in a narrow, upright format otherwise absent in his oeuvre. He retitled one of the surviving fragments *Two Figures* and the other *Portrait of a Dwarf*, 1975 (Private Collection, Australia). In *Portrait of a Dwarf* the cross-legged pose recalls both Velazquez's *A Dwarf Sitting on the Floor*, c.1645 (Prado Museum, Madrid) and the ancient Egyptian statue of Seneb, Chief of all the Palace Dwarves, which Bacon is likely to have seen in Cairo Museum in 1951.

Bacon's 'attendants' were cast either as voyeurs or as paradoxically disengaged witnesses of a horrifying spectacle, or of sexual intercourse. If, as I have proposed elsewhere, Bacon envisaged the homunculus as representing a Pygmalion figure (that is, a sculptor) and the convulsive figures as a Baconic variation of Galatea (a statue brought to life), it is comprehensible that he came to regard even this oblique allusion to the Greek myth as too 'illustrational'.

The two figures, closely intermingled (except for the heads they are virtually fused into one) in a glass cage, resemble a sculpture on display in a vitrine, albeit a conspicuously kinetic type of sculpture: one of the protagonist's legs actually bursts out of the cage structure. Bacon had inverted Cimabue's *Crucifixion* in his *Three Studies for a Crucifixion*, 1962, and he may have been performing a similar rotation, and a re-gendering of the figures, on one of many examples of the Galatea archetype.

62 UNTITLED (KNEELING FIGURE) c.1982

Oil on canvas · 198.0 × 147.5 cm
The Estate of Francis Bacon

In 1982 and 1983 Bacon began at least seven canvases, few of which he completed, that would have formed an extensive series of paintings of sculptures on plinths or pedestals.

All the sculptures were of severely truncated human forms. Among this group, *Untitled (Kneeling Figure)* most nearly resembles a monument on a plinth, although to judge from the phallic tassel that hangs above the figure, Bacon intended to locate the scene in an enclosed room space.

Ingres was a constant reference for Bacon's sculptural figures in this period. The right panel of a contemporaneous diptych, on a similar cadmium orange ground, titled *Study of the Human Body – from a Drawing by Ingres*, 1982, was based on Bacon's isolation of the lower body in the right-hand nude in Ingres' *Le Bain Turc*, and in 1983 he painted *Oedipus and the Sphinx after Ingres*. The torso in *Untitled (Kneeling Figure)* corresponds with the Sphinx in Ingres' *Oedipus and the Sphinx* (or, more specifically, to Bacon's abbreviated variant of it), and the extended leg may have been suggested by the pose of Paolo in Ingres' several versions of *Paolo and Francesca* and of Thetis in *Jupiter and Thetis*.

The foreground shadow anticipates the longer shadow Bacon employed in a closely related painting, *Still Life – Broken Statue and Shadow*, 1984, and both were variations of the shadow in a photograph of a father and daughter in a book that Bacon possessed of psychoanalytical essays, *L'Oedipe: Un Complex Universel* (1978).

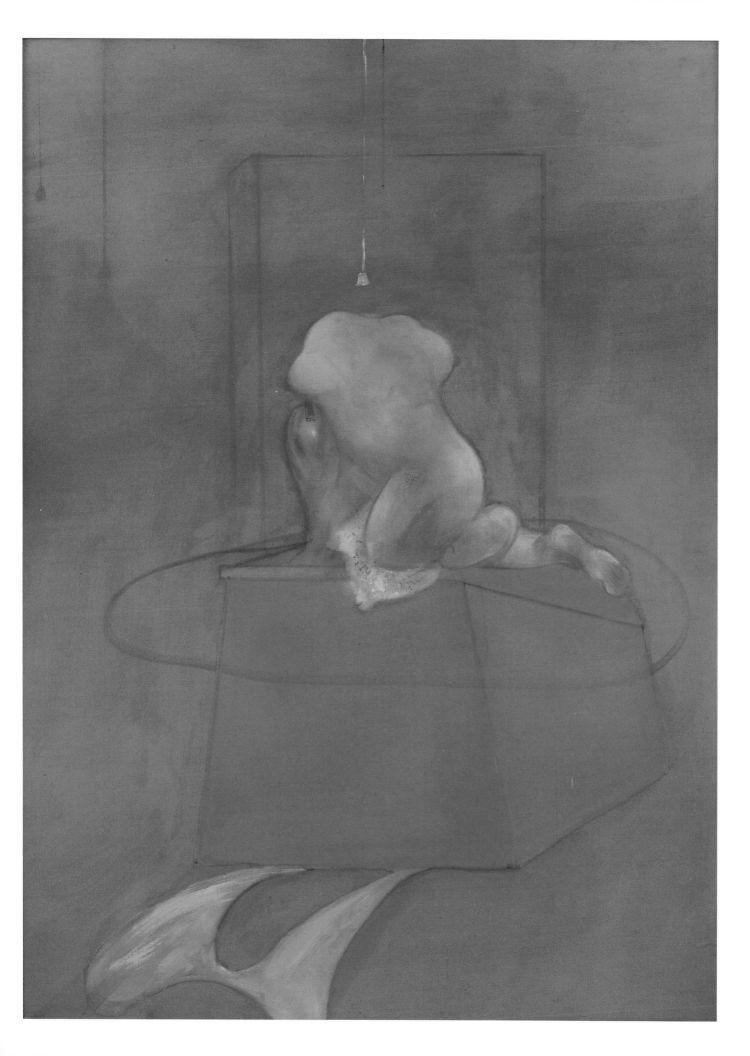

63 SECOND VERSION OF TRIPTYCH 1944 1988

Oil and alkyds on canvas · 198.0 × 147.5 cm (each panel)
Tate, London, presented by the artist, 1991

This reprise of the painting Bacon like to consider his 'Opus 1' accentuates, if anything, the inherent sculptural and monumental characteristics of the original, much smaller triptych of 1944. That it was a project of particular significance for Bacon, who was perhaps, at the age of seventy-eight, allowing himself to reflect on his artistic legacy, is emphasized by the scrupulous care he lavished on its execution.

The addition of a 'horizon line' places the images in a more perspectival 'room' than in the earlier version, although photographs of the outer panels in an earlier state show that Bacon decided to increase the two areas of black shadow in the foreground, thus minimizing the realism and recession of the table legs. The triptych has sometimes been compared unfavourably with its prede-cessor, but the deeper space reinforced the isolation of the mutilated, semi-human fragments, as though Bacon, later and more knowingly, intended the formal adjustment to intensify the psychological dimension of these hauntingly bony, eroticized, semi-human forms.

In comparison with the earlier version of the triptych, the much larger dimensions of the second version and the relatively open spaces of the outer panels draw attention to the enigmatic cropping of the forms, an aspect of the composition retained from the 1944 version. The addition of a rivetted clasp on the 'shoulder' of the central Fury is analogous with a repair to an old image, and the object on the 'floor' in the foreground of the left panel may be a related device that has fallen off the Fury, although it also resembles a 'discarded' slice of toast.

Second Version of Triptych 1944 was included in the exhibition *Francis Bacon* that toured the United States in 1989–90 (it was shown at the Hirshhorn Museum and Sculpture Garden, Washington, the Los Angeles County Museum of Art and the Museum of Modern Art, New York) and on its return it was loaned to the Tate. Bacon intended to make a posthumous bequest of the painting to the Tate, but he was persuaded to bring forward the donation and, on condition that there should be no ceremony to mark it, he gifted it to the Tate in 1991.

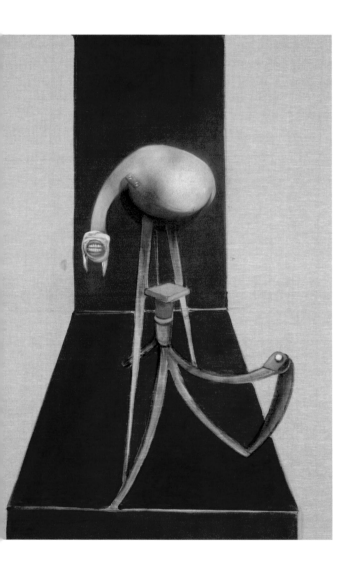 

Fig.56 | Francis Warner visiting Henry Moore
at Perry Green, 1975

Francis Warner

THE BONES AND THE FLESH:
HENRY MOORE AND FRANCIS BACON

It seems straightforward. Henry Moore was born a Victorian, the son of a coalminer in Castleford, Yorkshire, on 30 July 1898; Francis Bacon an Edwardian, in Dublin on 28 October 1909, of wealthy, countryhouse stock. Moore was loved, and to the end of his life talked tenderly of rubbing his mother's back to ease her rheumatism. Bacon claimed he was many times horsewhipped on his father's orders by young, unmarried grooms in the stables, and neglected by his mother.

Moore went to the local state schools; Bacon from 1924 to 1926 to the public school Dean Close in Cheltenham. Moore went on to Leeds School of Art and then the Royal College of Art where he later taught. Bacon claimed he had no art training. Moore was a strong and healthy man, happily married all his adult life, living at Perry Green in the country with Irena and their beautiful daughter; he was fascinated by, and later famously drew, sheep. Bacon was asthmatic, loathed animals and lived as a homosexual urban bachelor, mainly in London. Moore, conscientious and socially responsible, was on the board of many foundations. Bacon was relatively solitary, living in a mews near Harrods and moving in the shadows; Soho was his recreation and the underworld provided his friends.

Bacon's art depends on the ephemerality of the flesh, on sudden movement, the fleeting moment and its consequences. Moore disliked movement in sculpture: 'frisking, dancing figures and so on'.[1] 'A sculpture jumping off its pedestal is something I greatly dislike'.[2] He sought the timeless, the landscape, rocks, pebbles, bones, the structure of humans, the sleepers in the Underground.

Both artists repeated and honed their views and anecdotes for public consumption, Moore through years of teaching and press interviews, Bacon at the dinner tables and bars of London, and the baths and brothels of Tangier. The nation's tribute to the sculptor was 'a service of thanksgiving for the life and work of Henry Moore O.M., C.H., 1898–1986' in Westminster Abbey. The painter died suddenly, on a trip to Madrid to attempt to rekindle a relationship with a young man, on 28 April 1992. As he requested, there was no ceremony and no one was invited to the cremation.

But it is not straightforward. Indeed, the easy reduction of art to biography needs here to yield to a different orientation of thought; and context beyond the personal may provide a starting point. From our present (and passing) perspective, Moore and Bacon seem the last proponents of the Renaissance tradition: narrowing the timespan, the opposite end of the Pre-Raphaelite experiment – the completion of the spectrum shift which in part was precipitated by the discovery of photography. In the later Victorian era the prime focus was still on the supremacy of the human figure. Photography's tonal light and shade was driving artists to an emphasis on outline. This endorsed the contemporary need for clear demarcation, not least throughout the empire: the cornice dividing – not uniting – wall and ceiling, end-stopped rhymes in stanzaic verse, 'The rich man in his castle, the poor man at his gate', first – and third-class railway carriages (there was no second class). Photography was often shadowy, fuzzy, 'unwholesome', like any deviation from gender. Charles Collins' *Convent Thoughts*, 1851 (Ashmolean Museum), details the outline of every leaf and blade of grass, which is then filled in with colour. William Powell Frith's painting of the racecourse at Epsom, *Derby Day*, 1856 (Tate Gallery), renders a clearly recognizable portrait of every member of the vast crowd, each hat, shoe, fold and eyebrow. There is nothing impressionistic here. Everybody is doing something definite. He was the virtuoso of teeming life exactly detailed; Dickensian. To us the Pre-Raphaelite outline seems a last, sharp-edged rejoinder to photography's shadows, before representational art ceded that territory of visual record to emulsion on rolled strip.

Bacon and Moore are the mirror image at the opposite end of the same spectrum. The unquestioned assumption that 'The proper study of mankind is man' is the same, but his or her outline is not. Whereas for Collins one worked inwards from outline to enhance external recognition, the 'realism' of Moore and Bacon derives from the opposite perception.

Bacon loved poetry and plays, and Moore plays and poetry. Moore wrote and acted the lead in a play called *Narayana and Bhataryan* at Castleford Grammar School in 1920, dedicated to the memory of the poet Rupert Brooke. The play was heavily influenced by James Elroy Flecker, son of the founder headmaster of Dean Close School, who retired as Bacon arrived. Bacon knew the poetry of W.B. Yeats well, and would joust quotations with me. Moore designed the poster for the play I dedicated to him, *Meeting Ends*, and also generously designed the cover for an undergraduate magazine of *Oxford Poetry* for which I, as 'Senior Member', was finally answerable. Bacon would often quote W.B. Yeats' poem 'The Second Coming', written in January 1919:

> Things fall apart; the centre cannot hold;
> Mere anarchy is loosed upon the world.

Kathleen Raine introduced us to each other, and when he died she sent me her poem 'Remembering Francis Bacon', which includes the lines:

> At some party years ago you spoke to me
> Of Yeats, and of your sole desire
> Once, if only once, to touch the real.
> You were speaking from the heart.[3]

For Bacon, the 'real' was not the outline, but the centre, the inner heart of energy: 'Here the brushstroke creates the form and does not merely fill it in. Consequently, every movement of the brush on the canvas alters the shape and implications of the image.'[4]

Moore used to say:

The sculptor identifies himself with the object's centre of gravity, its mass, its weight; he realises its volume, as the space that shape displaces in the air ... One of the things I would like to think my sculpture has is a force, is a strength, is a life, a vitality from inside it, so that you have a sense that the form is pressing from inside trying to burst or trying to give off the strength from inside itself, rather than having something which is just shaped from outside.[5]

Talking of Giovanni Pisano, he said: 'Many early sculptors approached form from the outside ... but Giovanni was one of the first Italians to feel the bone inside the sculpture ... we could see how the elbow joints pushed out, that there was an inside structure.'[6]

Let us take two ways of looking at a tree. One is the army way, outline:

> There are three kinds of tree, three only,
> the fir and the poplar,
> And those which have bushy tops to.
> (Henry Reed, *Judging Distances*)

The other is to understand the outline simply as the point at which the energy growing up from the roots through the trunk peters out eventually in twigs. Yes, one can indeed join the tips of the twigs and notice that they make a beautiful arc, but the outline is not the explanation. One is a static way of thinking, the other dynamic. This is the trajectory travelled from the Pre-Raphaelite ideal to Moore and Bacon, before the concept and assumptions of art in our own time changed completely.

Both drama and poetry grow from the inside, as Moore the young dramatist (and later, from 1982, a member of the National Theatre Board) and Yeats-loving Bacon knew. Art, like religion or music, cannot satisfyingly be explained mechanically. They depend on movements of a nexus of mind, emotion, physical perception and intuitive insight. Focus on outline is inadequate. This motion is perhaps the essence of what it means to be alive. It is the inner life of things, rather than the beauty of colour or form, or even of significance or morality, that compels our complete attention: what Aristotle called 'giving life to lifeless things'. Our sense of wonder at a fine example is in part that we know such art can outlive the artist, and others unborn may respond the same way: with wonder.

If, in Victorian fashion, we begin from the outside, we note that as Bacon began to secure his reputation he insisted on presenting his pictures in the heavily gilded ogee frames made by Alfred Hecht of the King's Road, Chelsea. Their dimensions, weight of tradition, and resonances were important. They placed his work alongside the old masters. Both Bacon and Moore were preoccupied with the impact of size, in a way that the present computer-accustomed age may not immediately understand. To those born before computers became ubiquitous, size had a more immediate impact on the nervous system. Television presents us with a small, child-sized prattler, intruding into the well-lit private living space of a giant watcher who is in total control of extinguishing it; who can only be cajoled into allowing continued existence by, like Scheherazade on her wedding night, keeping the tyrant amused. Television by its very size invites the laughter of Lemuel Gulliver in Lilliput, where he found the inhabitants were six inches high. The Cheshire Cat grinned at Alice. The collapse of deference to politicians is in part due to their appearing on television – ingratiating, small, comic and expendable. We swat them with the remote control.

Film stars, by contrast, are larger than life. Our roles are reversed. In order to watch them in a cinema we must, like school children, leave home at a specified time to be checked, told where to sit, silenced and put in the dark: after a wait, remain for our allotted time gazing up at the gigantic figures who – unlike the attention-seeking child-puppets in our living rooms – take not the slightest notice of us. In wartime, picture palaces showed us Churchill, in the Pathé News reels, only on heroic scale. This Moore and Bacon well knew. Both tended to reject both television and film in favour of theatre, for two reasons, although early on Bacon had been inspired by Eisenstein and Buñuel. Theatre is a living, not recorded, art, unique, unrepeatable, like human life. No two performances are the same; and attempts to film stage shows fail. What is also true is that the actors are not only unpredictably living, but are our own size. As a result, as in normal daily life, if they speak to us they draw us in. If we applaud they smile; boo, they react. They are us.

So the painter and the sculptor – one in a static and the other in a dynamic way – always bore in mind the relationship of their potential work of art to the size of the spectator. Bacon's heavy and protecting frames deliberately contrast with the world of his depicted figures who are stark – anything but protected, imprisoned in their cubes and solitary rooms. Bacon, as a homosexual rejected and crimi-nalized by contemporary society, views society from the outside: from what he called his 'gilded squalor'. He knew our community to be for him non-commu-nicating, excluding, violent. So he makes his viewers stand beside him, join him, drawn to the reassuring traditional and hierarchical frames to peer into a view of our civilization that is anything but civil. As a result he is subversive. We, too, become outsiders, alienated from the world as he paints it. For his figures even pity seems inappropriate.

Henry Moore does not confine his sculptures. His ideal setting is the natural countryside with its ever-changing sky as backcloth. Though he shares with Bacon the view that the art object must be seen, and conceived, in relation to the size of the standing viewer, his is a dynamic approach in two ways. The advantage for the sculptor is that by walking around the object a viewer can see it from innumerable angles. Full appreciation is peripatetic. Jealousy of this advantage of sculpture over painting drove Picasso and Braque in 1911 to steal Mercator's technique and, by wrapping a grid around the object to bring all sides to the front as the paper was flattened out, gave us the creative distortions of cubism. Each large sculptural piece by Moore has its origin, its 'genesis', which grows from an embryonic form of a small, hand-held plaster maquette, usually based on natural forms, 'found objects' randomly encountered. These grow. I asked him if he hoped the final, full-sized sculpture would be the same as his maquette. He replied, 'One must always allow room for chance'.

For the Francophile Bacon, his retrospective at the Grand Palais, Paris, in 1971 was the most significant accolade he received: Picasso was the only living artist similarly honoured. At Bacon's invitation I attended the preview the night before the opening. We waited among the pictures, but uncharacteristically our courteous, punctual and genially enthusiastic host did not appear. We found this strange, until we learned next day that he had been detained to help the French police with their enquiries. George Dyer, Bacon's partner since 1963, had been found dead in their room at the Hotel St Pères, having taken an overdose of alcohol and barbiturates.

Grief's anguish can perhaps be fought by painting it, and the impact of *Triptych May–June 1973* is – by Bacon or anyone else – unrivalled. Here he directly faces what he believes are the consequences of his actions. Each black panel unflinchingly records Dyer's final moments. It is unadorned narrative; it reads from right to left. In the right-hand panel the naked, nose-bleeding George Dyer leans urgently over a basin, vomiting. The centre panel shows, under a bare bulb giving scarcely any light, Dyer's shoulder and head red and bruised above a waste pipe, his shadow forming a horned and spread-winged silhouette. By the third, his life has drained away, and his hunched, naked corpse slumps on a lavatory pan, its head fallen between the knees. It is the ultimate Bacon subject: the painter as model's murderer. The devilish shadow cast in the centre panel seeps from the waste pipe as well as from Dyer's body, and appears to be leaving the dying man to fly at the painter – or his substitute, the viewer. Death will claim us. Here is truth unequivocal.

In May 1985, at the opening of Bacon's second retrospective Tate exhibition, my seventeen-year-old daughter Lucy – later to become an artist not uninfluenced by Lucian Freud – accompanied me. Not having seen the label, she asked Francis whether his *Triptych – Studies of a Human Body* 1979, had a title. He replied mischievously with a quotation from T.S. Eliot's 'Sweeney Agonistes':

Birth, and copulation and death.
That's all, that's all.

Reading the triptych from viewer's right to left, it is true that the right panel shows a nude reclining male from the front, and the left the man with a new bullet wound bleeding through his back. The quotation also suits Bacon's final *Triptych 1991*, where the right panel shows the nude bottom half of a male body stepping towards us out of the darkness into light; on the left the same half body (both are surmounted by portrait photos) steps out of the light into the dark, genitals prominent. The centre panel of each of the two triptychs shows two entwined lying nude bodies. It was his final distillation of his view of life.

A third revisiting of the past is *Painting 1946 (Second Version) 1971*, which evokes *Painting 1946*. The *Second Version* changes the dominant colour, is more formal, calculated and tidier. It is just possible that I had a small part in provoking him to paint the *Second Version 1971*. In 1970 three one-act plays of mine, collectively titled *Maquettes* as they were small experiments for three larger plays, opened at the Oxford Playhouse, then later at the Edinburgh Festival on the Fringe. One, named *Lumen*, was a direct result of our conversations about the juxtapositioning of two carcasses of meat (as in *Painting 1946*) with – in my case – two human beings, in a context that sought to adapt cubism to the stage. It is not true to say Bacon designed our stage set, but he did encourage my experiment, seeing it for what it was: a tribute to him. He was intrigued. I was, in fact, drawing on my friendships with both artists, hoping to blend aspects of each into one stage metaphor. Moore's mastery of the archetypes extended to archetypal gestures. His bronze *Family Group*, 1948–9, height 152 cm, has had a mixed reception, but to me the view from behind, with its inexplicable tenderness of touch as the father places his hand on the mother's near shoulder, a gesture hidden from sight by their baby unless one walks round the back, is haunting. Is she supporting his heavy arm? Her neck shows no strain. Or is he lovingly supporting her? The ambiguity is perfectly balanced, and concentrates the power of Moore over our emotions at his greatest. It is not Michelangelo's spark of life across the fingertips of God and Adam, but something more mundane, understated, scarcely noticed.

An act of kindness to me by Henry was unexpectedly to benefit him, and had far-reaching consequences for good in my life. In 1970 Betty Tinsley sent a message at my Oxford college to say that Mr Moore had a visitor arriving from Canada. Would I be free and like to come to Perry Green to help entertain him? In retrospect I can see this was a friendly way of showing appreciation for the fact that I was dedicating the last of the trilogy of full-length plays, *Meeting Ends*, to him (Henry was to create its poster). The visitor was a Canadian in his early forties who from humblest Russian immigrant origins had built up a booming property empire in Toronto. His name was Albert Latner, the youngest and most brilliant of those 'merchant princes' of Prime Minister Pierre Trudeau's years turning Toronto from 'a hick town into a great metropolis', as its mayor, Philip Givens, put it. I knew two of Albert Latner's older mentors: Sam Zacks, financier, property developer and – with Ayala his wife – legendary art collectors. Each had the dedication of a play in *Maquettes*. Sam and Ayala, together with Albert Latner, Signy Eaton and her husband John of the department store chain, Edmund Bovey, President of the Northern and Central Gas Corporation, and a few others were to bring into being the Henry Moore extension of the Art Gallery of Ontario in Toronto four years later in October 1974. Henry invited both me and my daughter Georgina, aged eleven, to the opening. At the dinner he sat this youngest member of our party by the great Canadian photographer 'Karsh of Ottowa', who memorably told her how he had managed to capture the famous photograph of Churchill with fierce, bulldog expression by suddenly pulling the cigar out of his mouth and photographing.

On that original Perry Green afternoon in 1970, Albert Latner bought a bronze of *Three Motifs Against a Wall*, *1958*, followed later by the bronze *Reclining Figure*: *Angles*, 1979, to add to his and his wife Temmy's rapidly expanding collection of modern art. He also bought my production of *Maquettes*, and flew the whole company to Toronto for the North American première at Hart House Theatre in November, Samuel Beckett contributing his two tiny plays *Come and Go*, and *Breath*. Alan Schneider,

Beckett's North American stage director, directed all the plays. The press was favourable: Toronto was buzzing. Alan Schneider wrote to Beckett: 'The *Maquettes* I tried to make as simple and clear as possible, and the audience was most attentive. Mrs Zacks most pleased, and our friend Al Latner radiant in his first venture as producer.'[7]

Henry knew I would be there to see him committed to the earth. Nine months before his death my wife Penelope and I brought our baby Miranda to see him, who had for so long been a grandfather figure to my two elder daughters, my own father having died in 1955 at the age of fifty-one. Now for a few moments, as of old, a living mother and child was with him. As he looked down at the small face, his arm, his hands, protected our future; he had glimpsed a tremor of bliss, wide-eyed and contentedly sucking her thumb, and he wanted this happiness photographed. His last letter to me begins: 'Your book arrived safely and the photographs of Miranda with me – what a lovely baby she is, you must be very proud of her.' For his memorial service I wrote the Bidding Prayer of thanksgiving for his gifts, and asked that it be followed by the 'Introit' and 'Kyrie Eleison' from Mozart's *Requiem*. When we look more closely at one of the last great bronzes, *Mother and Child: Block Seat*, height 244 cm, we realize that instead of a nipple on the mother's breast there is a hole. Opposite is the baby, not with open mouth but with a protuberance to enter the hole. One day their roles will be reversed, the child will nurse the mother, and insert the feeding tube into *her* boneless gums: Moore's added major seventh to his final tonic chord.

This is an edited version of 'The Bones and the Flesh: Henry Moore and Francis Bacon' in Francis Warner, *Beauty for Ashes: Selected Prose and Related Documents*, Gerrards Cross, 2012, pp.141–184.

Acknowledgements

I am indebted to all my colleagues at The Henry
Moore Foundation, especially Anita Feldman, for
her insights into Moore and Rodin, Michael Phipps
for unearthing unpublished correspondence and rare
press cuttings in the Archive, and Emma Stower for
her advice in selecting images for this publication. I
would also like to thank Mary Moore for her interest
in the project from the start; Rebecca Daniels for
drawing my attention to a couple of obscure but
relevant Bacon references; and my friend and former
colleague Simon Wilson for his helpful comments
on the text.

RICHARD CALVOCORESSI

I am very grateful to all the private lenders of
Bacon's paintings. I also wish to thank Eddy Batache,
Elizabeth Beatty, Brian Clarke, Christophe Dejean,
Rebecca Daniels, James Dunnett, Carol Jacobi, Pilar
Ordovas and Hélène Pinet.

MARTIN HARRISON

Notes and References

Prologue · pages 10–13

1 The Burton Taylor Studio Theatre in the Oxford Playhouse is named after them.

2 Francis Warner, letter to Francis Bacon, 23 June 1969 (Marlborough Fine Art archive).

3 Francis Warner, *Beauty for Ashes: Selected Prose and Related Documents*, Gerrards Cross, 2012, p.261.

4 T.S. Eliot, *Collected Poems 1909–1962*, London, 1974 edition, p.131.

5 Henry Moore, diary entry for 8 March 1970 (Henry Moore Archive).

6 Michael Peppiatt, *Interviews with Artists 1966–2012*, Newhaven and London, 2012, p.186.

7 See Roger Berthoud, *The Life of Henry Moore*, London 2003, pp.375–6.

8 John Berger, 'A Sense of Touch', *The Guardian*, 21 September 1989, pp.25, 47.

Affinities · pages 15–29

1 Interview with John and Vera Russell, published in *Henry Moore*, exhibition catalogue, Marlborough Fine Art Ltd, London 1965, n.p.

2 John Goldsmith (ed.), *Stephen Spender Journals 1939–1983*, London 1992, p.229.

3 Ibid., p.235.

4 Ibid., p.383. Moore made four portrait sketches of Spender after their first meeting in 1934. He later designed covers for the magazine *Encounter*, of which Spender was founding co-editor, in 1961 and 1978 (for its twenty-fifth anniversary issue). In 1974 Spender wrote the text for an album of Moore's *Stonehenge* lithographs and in 1978 contributed a poem to Moore's album of etchings, *The Reclining Figure*. He gave the address at Moore's memorial service in Westminster Abbey in 1986.

5 Chris Stephens (ed.), *Henry Moore*, exhibition catalogue, Tate Britain, London 2010.

6 David Sylvester, *Henry Moore*, exhibition catalogue, Tate Gallery, London 1968, pp.36–8, 71.

7 See Roger Berthoud, *The Life of Henry Moore*, London 2003, p.302.

8 Ibid., p.199. See also Michael Peppiatt, *Interviews with Artists 1966–2012*, Newhaven and London 2012, p.186. Moore may have been having a dig at Bacon when he wrote in 1957: 'I do not really want to play the role of the obvious disturber. The bogyman business I leave to the Grand Guignol, to others. The crime and horror-comic line is theirs. I don't want to produce shocks' (from 'The hidden struggle', *Observer*, 24 November 1957; reprinted in *Henry Moore: Writings and Conversations*, edited and with an introduction by Alan Wilkinson, Aldershot 2002, p.119).

9 Berthoud 2003, op. cit. in n.7, p.302. Maurice Ash and his wife came to dinner with the Moores at Hoglands, Perry Green, on 5 June 1959 (Henry Moore Archive). This was after Bacon had left the Hanover Gallery but before his first exhibition at Marlborough Fine Art, Moore's London gallery.

10 Francis Warner in conversation with the author, Oxford, June 2013. According to Warner, Moore's reaction when he put the proposal to him was 'noncommittal'. Mary Moore, the artist's daughter, first told the author about Bacon's enquiry in 2010 but thought the intermediary might have been Stephen Spender.

11 Herbert Read, *Henry Moore Sculptor: An Appreciation*, London 1934.

12 James Beechey and Chris Stephens (eds), *Picasso and Modern British Art*, exhibition catalogue, Tate Britain, London 2012. See especially Christopher Green, 'Henry Moore and Picasso', pp.130–49.

13 Myfanwy Piper, 'Art', *Harper's Bazaar*, June 1963.

14 'New work by Henry Moore and Francis Bacon', *The Times*, 12 July 1963.

15 Nevile Wallis, 'Major occasions', *The Spectator*, 26 July 1963.

16 Bryan Robertson, 'Moore and Bacon', *The Listener*, 25 July 1963, p.127.

17 Andrew Forge, 'What art can encompass', *New Statesman*, 26 July 1963, p.120.

18 'Round the London galleries', *Apollo*, September 1964, p.240.

19 Bryan Robertson, 'Behind the pulpit', *The Spectator*, 13 August 1965.

20 Robert Melville, 'Garrulous extraverts', *New Statesman*, 30 July 1965.

21 John Russell, 'On bearable terms with the worst', *The Sunday Times*, 11 July 1965.

22 See Richard Calvocoressi, 'Moore, the Holocaust and Cold War politics' in Stephens 2010, op. cit. in n.5, pp.66–75.

23 Robert Melville Papers, Tate Archive: TGA 948 (uncatalogued). The author is grateful to Rebecca Daniels for drawing his attention to this passage.

24 Letter from Bryan Robertson to Henry Moore, undated but probably late 1959 (Henry Moore Archive). On 28 September 1959 Robertson invited Moore and his wife Irina to an informal, impromptu party for Sidney Nolan, who was arriving from New York and would be staying with him: 'K + Jane [Sir Kenneth and Lady Clark] are coming, Francis Bacon, all kinds of people + the room will be full of handsome, glamorous, sexy people, drinking unlimited drink. Do come – all we need are for you and Irina. And Nolan is a charmer'. As the Moores were leaving for Paris the morning of the party, they were unable to go but Henry replied by return: 'I am sure the party will be jolly good ... Give our love to everybody' (Henry Moore Archive). Nolan had exhibited at the Whitechapel in 1957.

25 Bryan Robertson, 'Preface' in *Henry Moore: Sculpture 1950–1960*, exhibition catalogue, Whitechapel Art Gallery, London 1960, n.p.

26 Alan Bowness, 'Introduction' in *Henry Moore: Volume 4, Complete Sculpture 1964–73*, London 1977, p.8.

27 Henry Moore in Wilkinson 2002, op. cit. in n.8, pp.228–9.

28 Sylvester 1968, op. cit. in n.6, p.5.

29 Ibid., p.127.

30 Ibid.

31 Ibid., p.128.

32 Ibid. The Henry Moore Archive contains letters from Sylvester to Moore outlining in detail his plans for the Tate exhibition. The proposal to use the lawn which runs parallel to the North Duveen Gallery for larger works, with access from the Rotunda via a specially constructed door and staircase, was suggested by the exhibition designer Michael Brawne and enthusiastically supported by Sylvester (letter from Sylvester to Moore, 20 June 1967). It was not Moore's idea, as stated in Berthoud 2003, op. cit. in n.7, p.400.

33 Henry Moore, 'The hidden struggle', op. cit. in n.8, pp.117–20.

34 See Christa Lichtenstern, *Henry Moore: Work – Theory – Impact*, London 2008, pp.146–150.

35 Kenneth Clark, *The Nude: A Study in Ideal Art*, London 1956, p.219. Moore's copy includes a typed message: 'Happy Christmas from Kenneth and Jane Clark'.

36 'Henry Moore: the Michelangelo vision', interview with David Sylvester, *The Sunday Times Magazine*, 16 February 1964; reprinted in Wilkinson 2002, op. cit. in n.8, pp.156–160.

37 David Sylvester, *Interviews with Francis Bacon*, London 1980, pp.83, 108ff.

38 Albert Elsen in collaboration with Henry Moore, 'Rodin's "Walking Man" as seen by Henry Moore', *Studio International*, July–August 1967; reprinted in Wilkinson 2002, op. cit. in n.8, pp.181–4.

39 Moore to Elsen, quoted in Wilkinson 2002, op. cit. in n.8, p.183.

40 Henry Moore in conversation with Alan Bowness, *Rodin: Sculpture and Drawings*, exhibition catalogue, Hayward Gallery, London 1970; reprinted in Wilkinson 2002, op. cit. in n.8, pp.176–80.

41 Moore also owned works by Courbet, Renoir, Degas, Seurat, Cézanne, Vuillard and Sickert. One of the two Degas drawings in his collection, a study of two dancers, is illustrated in Alan G. Wilkinson, *The Drawings of Henry Moore*, exhibition catalogue, Tate Gallery, London 1977, p.14, fig. 5. Bacon was not a collector although he did buy a double figure painting by Sickert, *Granby Street*, c.1912–14, from Anthony d'Offay, which he later gave to Lucian Freud.

42 Moore to Elsen, quoted in Wilkinson 2002, op. cit. in n.8, p.182. Moore was interested in how photography could enhance an understanding of sculpture, and for many years took photographs of his own work. Sylvester, for example, noted in the 1968 Tate catalogue that nearly all of its photographs were by Moore (op. cit. in n.6, p.vi).

43 Albert Elsen, 'Pioneers and premises of modern sculpture' in *Pioneers of Modern Sculpture*, exhibition catalogue, Hayward Gallery, London 1973, p.25.

44 Letter from Robert Sainsbury to Henry Moore, 24 April 1959 (Henry Moore Archive).

45 Letter from Robert Sainsbury to Henry Moore on Tate Gallery headed paper, 18 May 1972 (Henry Moore Archive). Sainsbury was instrumental in setting up The Henry Moore

Trust, which was eventually subsumed into The Henry Moore Foundation.

Bacon and Sculpture · pages 31–47

1 John Addington Symonds, *The Life of Michelangelo Buonarroti*, [London] 1893, vol. I, p.288.

2 David Sylvester, *Interviews with Francis Bacon*, London 1987, p.114.

3 Sylvester 1987, op. cit. in n.2, p.83.

4 Ibid.

5 Ibid.

6 Ibid., p.108.

7 Ibid.

8 Ibid., p.112.

9 Ibid., p.110.

10 Ibid., p.112.

11 Peter Beard interviewed by the author, New York, 5 April 2004.

12 Sylvester 1987, op. cit. in n.2, p.134.

13 Caravaggio could not, of course, have couched the creative process in photographic terms, even though it has been claimed he used a camera obscura. Roger Fry, who was ambivalent about Caravaggio, coincidentally raised a potential analogy with Bacon when he called him 'journalistic' and a potential 'impresario for the cinema': Roger Fry, 'Settecentismo', *Burlington Magazine*, October 1922, pp.158–69.

14 Commissioned by a papal lawyer, Laerzio Alberti, for his chapel in the Carmelite church of Santa Maria della Scala, Rome, the shocking realism of Caravaggio's *Death of the Virgin* nevertheless offended propriety and a less controversial substitute, painted by Carlo Saraceni, replaced it.

15 Norman Bryson, *Vision and Painting: The Logic of the Gaze*, New Haven, CT, 1983, p.92.

16 Ibid.

17 Sylvester 1987, op. cit. in n.2, p.114.

18 Ibid.

19 Ibid.

20 Ibid.

21 Ibid.

22 Ibid.

23 Unpublished passage in the transcript of David Sylvester's interview with Francis Bacon, October 1973 (Tate Gallery Archive).

24 David Sylvester, *Looking Back at Francis Bacon*, London 2000, p.248.

25 The unfinished marble for which this was a sketch is in the Accademia, Florence; the tomb itself, in much modified form, is in San Pietro in Vincoli, Rome.

26 'Survivors', *Time*, LIV, 21 November 1949, p.44.

27 Gilles Deleuze, *The Logic of Sensation*, [London] 2003, p.66.

28 John Rothenstein and Ronald Alley, *Francis Bacon*, London and New York 1964, p.52.

29 Anthony Zych interviewed by the author, Richmond upon Thames, 7 January 2007.

30 Michael Andrews and Victor Willing, 'Morality and the model', *Art and Literature* 2, Summer 1964, pp.49–64.

31 See Martin Harrison, *In Camera: Francis Bacon*, London 2005, pp.136–42.

32 Rodin quoted in Rainer Maria Rilke, *Auguste Rodin*, [London] 1946, pp.9–10. Rilke moved to Paris in 1902 to write this long essay, and for a while acted as Rodin's secretary. For an extended discussion of Bacon and Rodin, see Martin Harrison, *Movement and Gravity: Bacon and Rodin in Dialogue*, exhibition catalogue, Ordovas Gallery, London 2013, pp.4–39.

33 Michel Archimbaud, *Francis Bacon in Conversation with Michel Archimbaud*, London 1993, p.41.

34 Rilke 1946, op. cit. in n.32, p.17.

35 Hugh M. Davies, 'Interviewing Bacon, 1973' in Martin Harrison (ed.), *Francis Bacon: New Studies*, [Göttingen] 2009, p.104.

36 David Sylvester to Brian Clarke, 1998.

37 Grey Gowrie, 'The accelerated grimace', introduction to Bacon's exhibition at the Central House of Artists, Moscow, 1988 (in Russian); republished in English in *The Alligator* (an Oxford-based blog), 16 January 2009.

Moore catalogue entries · pages 49–105

1 'Notes by Henry Moore' in *Henry Moore*, exhibition catalogue, Tate Gallery, London 1951, p.3.

2 *Henry Moore: Writings and Conversations*, edited and with an introduction by Alan Wilkinson, Aldershot 2002, p.254.

3 Ibid., p.219.

4 Tate Gallery 1951, op. cit. in n.1, p.4.

5 Julian Andrews, *London's War: The Shelter Drawings of Henry Moore*, Farnham 2010, pp.48–9.

6 Kenneth Clark, *Henry Moore Drawings*, London 1974, p.120.

7 *Hall's Dictionary of Subjects and Symbols in Art*, with an introduction by Kenneth Clark, revised edn, London 1979, pp.302–3.

8 14 April 1945.

9 Moore/Wilkinson 2002, op. cit. in n.2, p.266.

10 David Sylvester, *Henry Moore*, exhibition catalogue, Tate Gallery, London 1968, p.109.

11 Tate Gallery 1951, op. cit. in n.1, p.16.

12 Moore/Wilkinson 2002, op. cit. in n.2, p.276.

13 Moore/Wilkinson 2002, op. cit. in n.2, p.284.

14 John Goldsmith (ed.), *Stephen Spender Journals 1939–1983*, London 1992, p.225.

15 David Sylvester, *Interviews with Francis Bacon 1962–1979*, London 1980, p.23.

16 Moore/Wilkinson 2002, op. cit. in n.2, p.284.

17 Sylvester 1968, op. cit. in n.10, p.127.

18 Roger Cardinal, 'Henry Moore in the light of Greece' in *Henry Moore in the Light of Greece*, exhibition catalogue, Basil and Elise Goulandris Foundation, Andros 2000, p.40.

19 *The Tate Gallery 1978–80, Illustrated Catalogue of Acquisitions*, London 1981, p.125.

20 Moore/Wilkinson 2002, op. cit. in n.2, p.285.

21 Clark 1974, op. cit. in n.6, p.228.

22 Sylvester 1980, op. cit. in n.15, pp.14–15.

23 Moore/Wilkinson 2002, op. cit. in n.2, p.129.

24 Ibid., p.130. Moore didn't count the 'Glenkiln Cross' as this was neither intentional nor a commission.

25 Sylvester 1980, op. cit. in n.15, p. 44.

26 Kenneth Clark, *The Nude: A Study in Ideal Art*, London 1956, p.245.

Bacon catalogue entries · pages 107–147

1 'Survivors', *Time*, LIV, 21 November 1949, p.44.

2 David Sylvester, *Interviews with Francis Bacon*, London 1987, p.8.

3 David Sylvester, *Looking Back at Francis Bacon*, London 2000, pp.91–3.

4 David Sylvester, *Interviews with Francis Bacon*, London 1987, p.37.

5 An extended analysis of the relevance of this imagery will appear in Amanda Harrison, *Circularities: Francis Bacon and W.B. Yeats*, forthcoming 2013.

The Bones and The Flesh · pages 149–154

1 Alan Wilkinson (ed.), *Henry Moore: Writings and Conversations*, Berkeley, CA, 2002, p.182.

2 Ibid., p.305.

3 Kathleen Raine, *Temenos 13*, London 1992, p.175.

4 Moore quoted in Michael Peppiatt, *Francis Bacon: Anatomy of an Enigma*, London 2008, p.182.

5 Moore quoted in Wilkinson 2002, op. cit. in n.1, p.184, 198.

6 Ibid., p.173.

7 Ed. Maurice Harmon, *No author better served: the correspondence of Samuel Beckett and Alan Schneider*, Harvard 1988, pp.236–40.

Image Credits